ON
SACRED
GROUND

Encountering the Great I AM
In the Midst of Suffering

Kate Kelty

Published by hope*books
2217 Matthews Township Pkwy
Suite D302
Matthews, NC 28105
www.hopebooks.com

hope*books is a division of hope*media

Printed in the United States of America

First paperback edition.
Paperback ISBN: 979-8-89185-216-7
Hardcover ISBN: 979-8-89185-183-2
Ebook ISBN: 979-8-89185-184-9
Library of Congress Number: 2025936260

Endorsements

"The beauty and power of this book is life-changing. Without patronizing words or 'pat answers,' the author shares her journey of raw pain and grief in seeking the depths of who God is to us. She writes with heart, soul, and intelligence. Every semester for eighteen years, my college students and I spend a week studying grieving and death. This is one of the best books on the subject. A must-read for Christians."

—Kay S. Walsh
Retired Adjunct Faculty, Psychology
Department, James Madison University

"*On Sacred Ground* is the book for those seeking to make sense of pain and suffering while holding onto the promise of a good God. These pages provide a perfect invitation to explore trust in God while facing some of the most difficult questions that can surface in the life of a believer. These words and this content provide an accessible, real-life framework for those looking for healing and peace while processing the questions of pain and grief. This book will strengthen the certainty of hope for anyone who reads it."

—Melissa Sloop
Pastor's Wife, Former Church Minister of
Families and Teens, Former Young Life Staff

"Tragedy, grief, and suffering are integral parts of the human experience. Regardless of your life journey, this book will resonate with all the deepest parts of you and bring comfort to your broken places."

—Pearl Hurst
Life Coach and Church Community Group Leader

"Kate's spirit-inspired words spoke to me in a way that validates and gives me permission to name my own painful experiences. The stories and first-hand God experiences Kate vulnerably shares encourage me to seek the deep comfort that only God can provide. In each I AM chapter, Kate reminds us that God gives hope and healing to carry me through life's certain suffering."

—Angie Strite
School Guidance Counselor

"When we suffer, sometimes our only comfort is knowing that Jesus first suffered for us. Kate Kelty's words offer a second comfort: there are people, imperfect and uncertain, walking among us who suffer, too, in their unique ways. We who hurt are not alone. And our suffering is not devoid of moments of peace, joy, and deep otherworldly comfort. This book proves that on so many levels."

—Ciara Brennan
Writer, James Madison University

For my faithful and beloved husband, Chris,
my precious—heavenly and earthly—children,
and for my beautiful Krissy, and all that you hold dear.

Table of Contents

Foreword

That's the direction you're invited to step towards, or at least lean into. No matter what grief you're enduring, it's time to move forward. One step forward. One breath forward. Forward at the pace of grace. That's the invitation being extended to you by my friend Kate Kelty in *On Sacred Ground*. You need to move forward, and you need someone to walk with you at the pace of grace.

The first time I "met" Kate, I was on an airplane. I was holding a manuscript that her dad had encouraged her to share with me. I don't think I was a full page into it before I was weeping. *The Jesus of my Grief* was intimate and desperate, honest and real. I found myself unable to stop reading—unable to stop crying. I became a fan of Kelty's writing and an even greater fan of her faithfulness in the valley of the shadow of death.

If you love, you will also grieve. The question is *how* you will grieve, and who you will be on the other side. Kelty grieves as one who knows the reality of hope. She's an honest friend on a journey no one wants to make, but everyone must.

If you're standing at the edge of grief—in singleness, infertility, depression, betrayal, rejection, abandonment, disease, or death—how will you move forward? Who knows the way? As a person who has grown familiar with the valley of the shadow of death, I attest to the need to walk with others. Yes, with the Good Shepherd, but also with sisters and brothers who know the way because they have been there themselves.... many times.

Betty was one of my guides on sacred ground. Betty had buried a son, and she could not find her way forward out of the grief. She sat for hours in the dark. And then one day, a friend encouraged her to move to the east-facing window. They sat there...in the dark...and then it happened: the first hint of light on the horizon. The first sound of the first bird. The first ray of a new day. Kelty knows the way to the Eastern-facing window in the dark, and she'll sit there with you until you can see light shining in your particular darkness.

As you read *On Sacred Ground*, you're going to think of the women who have traversed this ground before us. You're going to think of Eve and Sarah, Hannah and Mary. And you'll think of our brothers in Christ who have walked this sacred ground as well. You'll think of Moses and David, John and Paul. This is a book about all of them and none of them. A book about the 23rd Psalm and the disciples in the Upper Room, and the dismay we each experience on the road to Emmaus. It is a book about those journeys on sacred ground and the ones every believer has walked since.

If you're like me, there will be times that you cannot breathe and you have to put the book down because you can no longer see through the veil of tears, your hands wet from your own weeping. This is a book that you won't be able to put down. The fact that someone else understands your pain so deeply and has articulated feelings you've struggled to express is incredibly therapeutic. It fulfills a need that nothing else has been able to satisfy, leaving you wanting to absorb every last word.

Whatever your particular grief, welcome to the shared walk *On Sacred Ground*. We walk here together with a faithful friend who knows the way through grief, resilience, and joy. I confess the steps may be agonizing, and our conversations come in sighs and groans too deep for words.

Come, let's take a walk together. It's time to move beyond the *Forward*.

Carmen LaBerge
Author, Speaker, Radio Host

PART 1

To Suffer

I Am Suffering

"Because of God's tender mercy, the morning light from heaven is about to break upon us, to give light to those who sit in darkness and in the shadow of death, and to guide us to the path of peace."

Luke 1:78–79, NLT

"The winter prepares the earth for the spring, so do afflictions sanctified prepare the soul for glory."[1]

—George MacDonald

My life rolls like the Virginia hills: breathtaking peaks and devastating valleys. This life I sojourn in waves is nestled in the beautiful Shenandoah Valley of Virginia. I live on a cul-de-sac in a fifty-year-old, two-story brick home with a brand new front stoop and original cobwebs in every window. We are adjacent to Mennonite farms, and the clip-clop of nearby horses moves melodically, carrying people who cling to the past while living in the present. Our life is bursting at the seams. Our jobs, and our five children, keep us in a pace of hurry. But as the horses trot and the cornstalks sway steadily, I am reminded to live slowly. This frantic girl needs that reminder.

---

1   MacDonald, George. *Unspoken Sermons: Series I, II, and III.* Edited by Michael R. Phillips, Bethany House, 1985.

It's fall here, and I can't quite describe the beauty of mountain art in the third week of October. The sky is lit with autumn flames, and the trees begin their undressing; a graceful shedding of harvest hues dotting the green earth. I reflect that even that which falls can be stunning. This faltering girl needs that reminder.

Soon, the soft golden blanket of earth will turn a crackling brown, and all will become dull, and the afternoon sky will grow dark. Not even our valley can hide from that. Naked branches will reach skyward, a reminder that reaching is the right thing to do when all has been lost. This frail girl needs that reminder.

The kitchen table (my writing desk) is situated in the sunroom and lit with morning rays. I look up and smirk at the dozens of dirty little fingerprints on the window panes. I am a fickle feeler, both irritated and endeared to these messy masterpieces and the fingers that made them. My gaze is interrupted by a group of wind-tossed leaves succumbing to a game of tag. I can almost hear a chuckle as they race past the window and around the house. I suddenly feel fortressed by the thought that death doesn't dissuade joy. As the tree weeps its leaves, a eulogy of goodness and grief falls to the earth and to me. I watch it unfold outside my window, both enchanted and anguished by the gracious descent I know all too well.

My gaze deepens to the farm behind our yard, a true panoramic masterpiece. Three flaming pear trees wave. I smile in response. The silo stands tall and proud behind them. Its job is by far the easiest on the farm and yet the most important. He is the holder, the provider of grain when winter fields cease to yield. A thought rises: *it's time to store up words for winter, truth for the meager months ahead.* A season of paltry portions is coming, but there is a silo within. I will not go hungry. This famished girl needs that reminder.

I look down to see that exactly five copper leaves from the towering oaks in our backyard snuck in with the dog. They lay scattered under the table along with Max, who lies long and shaggy at my feet. I can't decide if I'll pick up the leaves and throw them away—or if I should name them. Should I memorialize this foliage that might have fallen from me? They are lifeless but lovely, so for now, I leave them, just like the fingerprints. Today, I make space for the messes that match the messy in me. These October guests, or perhaps intruders, hint that some things shuffle in, invited or not. Winter comes after fall every year, just like grief comes for me. It's an annual arrival, my February flu, and I know I will be laid bare like the tree, browned like the earth, and claimed by the cold. It is also grief that gives me flickering fires, blanket forts, and warm sips that go straight to the soul. Grief may trap me, but she also embraces me. We are frenemies. I am reminded that grief has a good side, and this frightened girl needs that reminder.

This upcoming February, my grief reaches a significant milestone. My grief turns eighteen. On February 25th, 2005, my fully formed baby girl died within me. I have loved her, longed for her, and grieved for her every day since. I wish I were planning the most epic birthday celebration for Anna, with a graduation party a few months after that. But this is not my reality. Instead of raising Anna, I've raised grief. Instead of nearly two decades of memories with our girl, I have memories of mourning her absence. I remember all the places I've wept for her over the years. I remember *that* couch. I remember *that* parking lot. I remember *that* store. I remember the hundreds of times I nearly drowned in my own bed.

The seasons of sadness haven't been for my daughter alone. I've been impaled with grief for my twenty-three-year-old brother-in-law, who was fine one moment and gone the next. I've wept wretched tears for my lifelong friend lost to cancer, my final baby to miscarriage, and a son whose spectrum of challenges breaks my heart daily. This is the grief that comes with loving.

But what about the grief that comes from being lied to? The flaming arrows of the deceiver strike and stun, and I forget both *who* I am and *whose* I am. There's also the grief that comes in relationships, when trust is broken, when flippant words slap, and when what once felt safe is now treacherous. There's the grief of sickness, when engines are struck with disease and the body sputters and the heart breaks. So many winters of weeping have come for me. So many wondrous moments with the One who lit the matches, provided the blankets, and gave the warm cups of living water to thaw and soothe. I am held together knowing a losing life is a gaining life. This fragile girl needs that reminder.

In anticipation of this eighteenth birthday and my sorrow coming of age, I process how I will honor both my girl and my grief. I need it to be significant because *they* are both so significant. But even our pink balloons feel too sad this year. The desire to wrap my arms around her neck, to hold her face and look into her blue eyes, to tell her how proud I am of her and how ready she is for the world, is almost too much to bear. I miss the conversations we never had. I long for the laughs we never shared. I ache for the songs she never sang. I stare at the emptiness and almost feel poor. But then my eyes are opened, and shack walls give way to marble staircases and chandeliers drip with crystal prisms, casting rainbows of provision on every wall. The God that made me poor is making me rich. A voice rises from the valley of the shadow of death and wraps any remaining angst in the promise that "surely goodness and mercy shall follow me all the days of my life: and I will dwell in the house of the Lord forever" (Psalm 23:6, KJV). I am consumed with assurance and joy, reacquainted to the miraculous power of remembrance. This forgetful girl needs that reminder.

I stand up from the kitchen table in search of my sweater. The day is growing colder. I walk to the faux wood stove in the corner of the room. I turn it on, instantly mesmerized by the fake flames. They flicker, and something inside flickers, too. The heat isn't blowing yet, but I am already warming from the promise of warmth. I ponder the miracle of the moment, that getting warm always begins with looking to the source of warmth, our true flame. In fact, the first time God tells us His name, He is enveloped in flames. He greets Moses in his desert hiding place, and from within a burning bush, He speaks. God told Moses to take off His shoes, that the ordinary ground he walked on was sacred and holy (Exodus 3:5). With empathy and authority, He exudes, "I have surely seen the affliction of my people who are in Egypt and have heard their cry because of their taskmasters. I know their sufferings, and I have come down to deliver them…" (Exodus 3:7–8, ESV). God asked Moses to return to Egypt, to His beloved captive Israelites, and to tell Pharaoh to let His people go. When Moses asked who it was that conversed with him, God told him His name (Exodus 3:10–14). This was an epic moment. Previously, God was referred to by the Hebrew title *"Elohim"*. But now, He was revealing His name: *"Yahweh."* It means, *"I AM that I AM"* (Exodus 3:14, ESV). It means I exist. No one created Me. No one sustains Me, and no one is greater than Me. He was saying, quite literally, with one word, My existence will be your deliverance.

Yahweh was also a trump card. The Egyptians worshiped categorical gods, including the god of the sun, fertility, and war, to name a few. Yahweh was a name that absorbed all other titles; a name meaning, 'I AM' God of all things and all people for all time.

It takes my breath away that the catalyst for God to reveal the intimate identification of His name was the suffering of His children. This God is not only drawn to His children when they hurt, but He is a Deliverer who wants to be known.

I love this intimate and inspired description of I AM in the first three verses of Isaiah 61 (NLT):

> The Spirit of the Sovereign Lord is upon me,
>
> for the Lord has anointed me
>
> to bring good news to the poor.
>
> He has sent me to comfort the brokenhearted
>
> and to proclaim that captives will be released
>
> and prisoners will be freed.
>
> He has sent me to tell those who mourn
>
> that the time of the Lord's favor has come,
>
> and with it, the day of God's anger against their enemies.
>
> To all who mourn in Israel,
>
> he will give a crown of beauty for ashes,
>
> a joyous blessing instead of mourning,
>
> festive praise instead of despair.
>
> In their righteousness, they will be like great oaks
>
> that the Lord has planted for his own glory.

The word for Lord in this text is Adonai, a reverent nickname for Yahweh. God's people so revered and feared His true name that they spoke and wrote "Adonai" in order to keep "I AM" sacred and holy. Isaiah's prophetic words give clarity regarding centuries of circumstances; we will be both pierced by and imprisoned to the world. In this passage, we are rightly named broken-hearted captives. But Adonai is also named the Comforter, the Rescuer, and the King. By this, God, and through Him, we become the comforted, the freed, and the righteous. This passage is a Messianic prophecy, foretelling Yahweh's arrival as King to save His sons and daughters.

Centuries after Yahweh revealed His name, He finally revealed His face. In John 8, Jesus addresses the teachers of the law and the Pharisees in a maddening conversation. The religious men refuse to believe Jesus and challenge every word He speaks. They call Him a demonized lunatic. But with one final rebuttal, Jesus removes the proverbial cloak of a humble Jewish teacher, revealing His sovereignty. He boldly announces, "Truly, truly I say to you, before Abraham was, I AM" (John 8:58, ESV; emphasis added). The enraged Pharisees immediately set to stone Him. How dare this Nazarene take Yahweh's name. Blasphemy. But it was this same humble Jew who spoke to Moses from within the blaze centuries before. Jesus seeks to bring the frigid Pharisees fireside with the truth of Himself revealed. From the desert flames to Israel's frontier, behold, I AM. They couldn't see that this ragged nomad before them was in fact the visible image of the invisible God they feared, the King they waited for. So, they rejected and reviled Him. They didn't get to know the warming and transforming power of I AM. But Mother Mary did, as well as beloved John. Close behind was betraying Peter and murderous Paul, followed by centuries of saved sinners and now, me. I believe in every pitiful "I am" we profess, His powerful "I AM" can change everything. When I moan, "I am weary," He sympathizes, "I AM your rest."

When I cry, "I am wounded," He declares, "Beloved, I AM your healer."

When I weep, "I am alone," He whispers, "Child, I AM ever present."

Every perfect quality of Father God says something beautiful, possible, and miraculous for and about us. The chapters ahead are my naked, cold, and shivering "I am" wrapped into the gentle, warm, and flaming arms of *the* I AM.

His name is "Being." I breathe deep and climb into this warm word, a bath. By this name, this divine holding, I am both cleansed and soothed. It is within His Being that I live and breathe and find my own being (Acts 17:28). His gift to those of us who call Him Father is a family heirloom, a crown in exchange for ashes, a gift only to be bestowed on those whose DNA matches His own. On the biting days, I feel certain the winter will kill me, and the ones I suffer with and for. It's a cold war we fight in hearts, homes, offices, hospitals, and even churches. There is no hiding from winter. Not for me, and not for the ones I love most. Not for...

> My friends who wrestle under the isolating devastation of infertility.
>
> My friends who long for soul mates and weep in the waiting rooms of singleness.
>
> My friends who suffer from spiritual, psychological, and sexual abuse and subsequent trauma.
>
> My friends who feel unknown and uncared for by their spouses.
>
> My friends who wake in the darkness of depression, begging for the light of Jesus.
>
> My friends who are widowed—grieved and worry about what the future holds.

My friends who are divorced and feel the torment
of misunderstanding and shame.

My friends who fight weary against tumors, mass-
es, and despicable diseases.

This list is not comprehensive. This is a short list of those
closest to me. We truly are broken-hearted captives of this world.
The circumstances of our suffering may be different, yet the same
painful thoughts and feelings imprison, bully, and beat us up in
our personal Egypt. If we listen carefully, we will hear our names
being called by God, just as Moses did from the burning bush in
Exodus: Take off your shoes, beloved, this ground that hurts you
is holy. I am deeply concerned for your suffering, and I hear your
cries. You belong to me, and I AM your Yahweh.

As I sit here in my messy sunroom in the chill of my own
grief, I wonder, how cold are you, rolling traveler? In what ways do
you suffer? What evil tempts you, and what questions taunt you?
*Will I feel like this forever? Does God really care about me? How can I
trust Him when He allowed my pain?* For every question, He is the
answer. For every tear shed, He is our compassionate companion.
For every broken heart, He is the mighty mender. For every battle
fought, He is our confident champion. Jesus is our sovereign, sympathetic Savior. He is the blaze and the Word. He is the warmth
and the light. He is burning bright in front of you. He is burning
bright *for* you. He is I AM, and there isn't a soul on the earth without the need of this Redeemer.

A naked branch raps at the window. Birds overhead sing as
they head south for the southern heat. The draft creeps in through
the window cracks, and I wrap myself tighter in the blanket around
my shoulders. Yes, winter is coming. The fire is lit. It crackles and

speaks to Moses, to you, and to me. Come in from the cold. Come into the warmth. Come encounter I AM with me.

Oh Jesus, my Jesus, Your very being is what I need as I suffer. You are Yahweh. You are the everything I need to be released, redeemed, and restored. I cry out to You in the agony of the lies I believe, the losses I have endured, and the life I live, exhausted and afraid. I need the truth about You to know the truth about me. Burn bright in my desert of despair. Open my eyes to see You and my ears to hear You. Make this suffering ground sacred ground. I am Yours, I AM.

PART 2

To Know

CHAPTER TWO

I Am Present

"I can never escape from your Spirit! I can never get away from your presence! If I go up to heaven, you are there; if I go down to the grave, you are there. If I ride the wings of the morning, if I dwell by the farthest oceans, even there your hand will guide me, and your strength will support me. I could ask the darkness to hide me and the light around me to become night, but even in darkness I cannot hide from you…"

Psalm 139:7–12, NLT

"For He is our endless bliss, and He made us for Himself alone, and restored us by His blessed passion, and keeps us in His love, and will never suffer us to be lost. For He is ever with us and never leaves us."[2]

—Julian of Norwich

On February 22, 2005 I paced and prayed. The hospital floor was cold against my bare feet, winter knocking for entrance with the aim of my soul. But in the very center of me, hope burned strong, chasing worry away. I clutched my belly, nine months ripe, and though my girl had been still for hours, I knew she was tucked sleeping and safe inside. The God I loved and leaned on would not fail or abandon me. The God I trusted didn't

---

2   Julian of Norwich. *Revelations of Divine Love*. Translated by Elizabeth Spearing, Penguin Classics, 1998, p. 79.

let fully formed babies die in their mothers' wombs. The doctor would arrive in moments and excuse the cold fear now banging for entrance. Chris broke the silence, first with his simmering eyes, a message of loudest love, and then with his words, "Kate, whatever happens, we will be okay."

I was appalled. How dare he even consider an outcome other than life? How faithless was he? I pulled away from his suggestion and subsequent comfort and toward the necessity for hope. Our God would not let us down. But Chris already knew what the doctor would soon proclaim. He wasn't faithless. He was faith full and ached for his wife to be prepared for what would be taken, and what couldn't. The doctor placed the wretched probe on my belly, revealing four perfectly formed and precious chambers of a placid heart. His "I'm sorry" struck my mind and soul like a lightning bolt to the ground. My solid foundation cracked wide open, and from this ravine came screams of horror, sounds I had never uttered before. Instinctively and emphatically, I called for Jesus over and over. It wasn't too late! Death was just an invitation for His power, right? The doctor, compelled by compassion, placed the probe on my abdomen once more. But nothing changed, except for my confidence in the presence, power, and goodness of God. The screaming for His name was replaced by the wails of a shocked and grieving mother. I searched my favorite eyes for an answer, but Chris was just as grieved as I was. Anna was gone… and so was Jesus. I felt abandoned by God in that hospital room, now covered in ice and winter. I wouldn't have said it that way at the time. But that is what my soul sought to conclude.

The hospital was my wretched home for the next several days. I waited and wailed in preparation for my baby to be delivered and taken from me. I longed for the comfort of God's presence, and yet

I was equally afraid of Him. The vast hole His perceived absence created was quickly filled by our families and friends. My big sister Kristen climbed into my hospital bed and wept against me. My best friend Montica fixed herself to my side, though it took her breath away. Laura's compassionate calm held my panicked gaze and reassured me on a path of grief she had also been forced upon. Karla's gentle hands rubbed my belly, though what lay beneath would never know her nurture. Nine months of carrying, feeling, praying, singing, and loving Anna Rose were now shockingly over. I vacillated between sobs, screams, and frozen stares. I carried a fully formed, lifeless child who would soon be delivered into my trembling arms. I was pained and petrified, and they were present. My dearest friends were comforters when I couldn't feel the presence and comfort of God.

There is nothing quite like the love of a safe other amidst suffering. In fact, that is exactly what comfort means: to suffer with. The presence of these sisters changed nothing in my world, but much in my heart. I didn't know how I would survive without Anna. I didn't know how to live in the wilderness of grief, but I did know who would be with me.

My greatest suffer-with companion was Chris. It was his warm hands on my wet cheeks and gray-blue eyes locked with mine that comforted and consoled. When my sobs began to suffocate and breaths were hard to find, his tender love reminded me there were deeper breaths inside. Not a single word needed to be spoken. In fact, not a single word could be spoken. Nothing could possibly be said to ease the pain. Chris was present, and that was enough, until it wasn't. Eventually, he went back to work, and I was completely alone except for the cruel company of my grief. That first morning without him was brutal. I wept on the floor in Anna's hollow nursery, my sorrow escalating until pain became panic. I couldn't breathe. I started hyperventilating. I needed Chris. I needed my companion. I hadn't endured a moment like this without him, but he wouldn't be home for hours. In sorrow and desperation, the soul begs for its true companion. Though my mind fought against the urge to pray, a needful plea emerged. This plea didn't even seem to belong to me. It was so vulnerable and etched in faith, I thought I'd lost. Buried deep under the rubble of my grief, belief was intact, and it had a voice:

"Jesus help me!"

I didn't expect a reaction or a response. Even if God was listening from afar, why would He come to me now, especially after so many months of seething in anger and blame? Though I felt justified in my feelings, I was deeply ashamed. Though the "abandoned" argument was strong, I knew deep down my belief in Him and devotion toward Him were not entirely lost. I didn't deserve His presence or kindness, but then, the still quiet voice presented the most tender of whispers in my left ear: "I'm here." A sudden and deep breath surfaced in my lungs. I released it slowly. I took in another deep breath, and fear and doubt vanished. It was as if someone was both breathing and feeling within me. These breaths and emotions were not mine, and yet they were. I was suddenly and supernaturally delivered from panic to peace, and there was only one explanation: I was in the presence of God. Another deep breath came—another liberating release. There was no doubting it. Jesus was here, and even more significantly, I knew He always had been. It was deep knowing, like a burning ember under the smoldering ash heap. Though the accuser condemned Him to me, a cruel deadbeat, I knew the truth. My Father didn't just arrive at my desperate plea, no; He had never left me. This awareness didn't haul all the ashes of confusion and pain away, but it did give the answer my lonely soul craved: my God had never abandoned me. His presence was the ember within. I stayed on the floor for an hour. I didn't dare move. The nursery was no longer an empty space. It was a sanctuary. The very room of Anna's absence became the haven of His presence. The enemy's lie that tricked me into believing God had vanished was now dispelled. In crisis, we are squeezed and birthed anew into the cruel world of suffering. We cry out helplessly. Just like a cold and scared newborn baby, we begin searching. Who is here to swaddle me, to comfort and feed me? Who can I trust? What voice is that? A warning voice? A finger pointer in this mess and madness. Father God left you, says the father of lies. Distrust suddenly feels reasonable. Fear feels necessary. Deception feels like… the truth.

Can you relate? Has your vulnerable soul ever been deceived amidst suffering?

The enemy of our lives prowls around like a roaring lion looking for those to devour (1 Peter 5:8). A suffering soul is weak and easy prey. Jesus, understanding the enemy and the human heart, seeks to prepare and equip His followers before His death rattles them. This preparation is also a living and active promise and provision for you and me. It is both a balm and a lantern: "I will not leave you as orphans…" (John 14:18, NIV).

Do you hear the urgency in His promise? The desperation even?

This is the voice of the Father that begs to be clung to when suffering strikes. Jesus knew what nightfall would bring. He knew His closest companions would be impaled by grief and vulnerable in their confusion, pain, and fear. He knew the accuser, an impostor father, would tempt them to believe they had been deserted by the One they trusted to be their Savior. Jesus, knowing all of this, lays out His words; a living, sustaining meal. What a resolute, tenacious, and tender promise from a fiercely loving Father to His beloved boys: "I will not leave you as orphans." He knew His death would make them feel like a band of terrified lost boys. His promise was a feast of hope, security, and identity given to consume and savor when they found themselves alone and afraid.

Now listen to Jesus' words again, but this time, hear them for yourself…

"I will not leave you as an orphan."

The echo and power of words spoken long ago to reassure and anchor still reverberate in the canyons of our loss and fear.

Just a few verses later Jesus gifts His promise to His disciples (and to us) again: "But in fact, it is best for you that I go away, because if I don't, the Advocate won't come. If I do go away, then I will send him to you" (John 16:7, NLT). What was Jesus saying? How could anyone be better than the Messiah, the One all of history had longed and waited for? Yet now Jesus declares that His departure will make way for another who will be best for them. His name is Advocate (paraklētos), meaning helper and comforter.[3] The disappearance of Jesus made way for His reappearance as the unseen "be-with" God, flowing with all help and consolation. This was Jesus in a form that could constantly soothe the soul. This is the power of the Spirit, and the very reason Jesus wanted His disciples to understand why it was good for Him to go. Emmanuel with them would now become Emmanuel within them. He knew the deep grief that was before them, and He knew they would need to be comforted from the inside out, from the place where pain

---

3   Strong, James. *Strong's Exhaustive Concordance of the Bible.* Thomas Nelson, 1990. Entry G3875.

originates and dwells. While the Messiah's power had limits by His physical form, the Spirit has no bounds, and there is no wait time for the Comforter to arrive. He is everywhere, always. He is in hospital rooms and on nursery floors; He is in every corner of this world and every crevice of a shattered heart. The presence of God is the comfort of God. The noun cannot be separated from the verb. They are one and the same, and the Spirit makes it a permanent reality in the souls of those who call upon His name. We cannot experience the glorious comfort of Jesus without truly understanding, seeking, and cherishing His embedded presence as the Holy Spirit. He is our one and true suffer-with companion.

It all sounds good and true, but suffering smothers like a wet blanket, making it nearly impossible to feel anything but the cold and heavy weight of misery. Additionally, when darkness hides His face, the enemy holds the shovel and heaps piles of deceptive ashes onto the ember of our hope and faith. The ember must be fanned into flame. The oxygen for the fire to grow is simply our panting breaths confessing need. It's as simple as "Jesus help me," whispered full of doubt to the God who burns within.

Have you whispered this plea in a space emptied of your hopes and dreams? Have you wanted to cry out to Him, but stopped, silenced by doubt and fear?

Perhaps your pain was caused by a death, or maybe it was damage inflicted upon you by another. Maybe you know the punctures of being emotionally or physically hurt or even abandoned by a parent? By a beloved? Maybe your suffering is constant physical pain or the heavy burden of someone you love. Whatever the pain, the God we cannot see, and maybe cannot feel, is with us. Can you muster a whisper through all the warring messages of doubt, hurt, and blame? How can you find the courage to call upon His name?

The pain that makes us heave the silent sobs and the guttural wails is a language made by Him and for Him. Our pain is the soul's deep request for the companionship of a holy and healing God, and our condemnation of Him doesn't change who He is or how He feels about us. He gave us His name centuries ago when we were abandoned and abused in Egypt. He told us then He was our everything. He showed us His presence and His power in a burning bush to Moses and then as a fire by night to guide His wandering children. Then He became the walking flame of Jesus on earth, the One who said, "...I AM the light of the world..." (John 8:12, ESV; emphasis added). And now, He is the furnace within. He is in-dwelling I AM. He is the heat that thaws, the fire that ignites, and the light that guides our way. The evil of winter is no match for the internal, radiating warmth of the Holy Spirit of God. He has heard every cry we have ever made, even the ones yet to be wept. He is the Present One, and though that may not change our circumstances, it can undoubtedly and unreservedly change our souls. It all starts with an ember: Jesus, our ever-present Comforter.

Twenty years ago, I called my big sister Kristen on the way to the hospital to ask her to pray for us and for Anna. She was the only person I called. I told her I'd not felt my baby girl move in hours. After she hung up the phone, she begged God to spare Anna's life. An hour passed, and she had still not heard from me. She was beside herself. She sat down to do her Bible study, and the Scripture for that day was 2 Corinthians 1:3–4 (NLT), which reads: "All praise to God, the Father of our Lord Jesus Christ. God is our merciful Father and the source of all comfort. He comforts us in all our troubles so that we can comfort others. When they are troubled, we will be able to give them the same comfort God has given us."

At that moment, Kristen was seized with panic. She allowed herself to wonder for the first time, is my niece actually gone? Has my little sister's baby died? She stared at the Scripture before her and knew God had prepared her for what was ahead for our family, both in grief and comfort.

She hadn't shared this moment with me for years. She knew I needed to be so deeply and thoroughly comforted by God before the knowledge of becoming a comforter to others would bless me. When we suffer with the Spirit again and again, a quilt of moments is stitched one by one until a blanket of comfort—a "comforter"— exists. It's our testimony to the presence of God. And now it's ours to share, to wrap around the shoulders of our shivering friends who are doubting but desperate for the presence and comfort of God. We become the gift givers. With confidence in Jesus' promise from John 14:18, we can say to the suffering friend: He has not left you as an orphan. Your Abba is here.

As I write this morning, I am deeply engaged with the timeline of my own suffering—the losses and pains of my life resolved, and those still standing. I also hold in my heart the many brothers and sisters I love who are walking and weeping in the darkest valleys. I think of them, and I also think of you. I am so deeply sorry for every moment of suffering you have endured, every moment when your pain and the enemy's lies have led you to believe you have been abandoned by the truest Lover of your soul.

It hurts to live, doesn't it? It is also the dearest of blessings to receive comfort. Jesus said it so plainly in His sermon on the mount, the one where He flips the "blessed" man upside down: "Blessed are those who mourn, for they will be comforted" (Matthew 5:4, NIV). There is a certain abundance that is given to those in the poverty of pain. I can testify to the magnificence of being rescued by His presence just as much as I can testify to the misery of suffering. I've often wondered on this forty-five-year journey with its many trips through the Valley of Despair, would I give it up? Would I trade my "blessing" for a life without pain? As shocking as it is to say, I choose my blessing. I choose the precious and powerful presence of God in my suffering and sacred valley over a life outside of it. The Valley is no longer the place I growl in, but the place I groan in with a dependence that leads to joy. Over time, as I have practiced His presence and inclined my ear to His voice, the Spirit's comfort has grown from single words to short phrases to whole conversations. His Word has become a glorious novel, and His whispers are intimate treasures. Jesus longs to share the secrets of His heart with dependent children. The comfort of God is intimacy with God. Suffering is often the catalyst to knowing God's presence because we need it so desperately. But when the suffering is over, the memories of the intimacy that were born in suffering remain, and so does the longing for more of Him. We can take the awareness of His presence and the dependence we came to know and love in the night, right with us into the dawn of a new morning. The intimacy we were made for with our Father begins and ends with His presence. I long for your ember to be ignited by the truth that the sweetest and mightiest Savior is with you. I also ache for hope—that you will know with escalating joy and anticipation that your pain is not the end of your story. Comfort that soothes, satisfies, and begs to be given is yours. I know that might not feel desirable today amidst your suffering. But it's not a transaction of the cruelest pain for a consolation prize of comfort. It's a flow of the deepest grace and goodness that weaves our stories of stabbing pain into satiating joy and beautiful, remarkable blessing. We are not orphans. We are Abba's kids, and we will never be left alone.

Dearest Father and ever-present friend, You are here. Your Spirit is the ember and the flame that I am desperate for. Take away the fear and accusation that You are against me and have left me as an orphan. I cry out to You with unresolved fear and anger, "Jesus help me." "Jesus, I need you." "Jesus, please save me." Let me know the power of Your presence and the precious companionship I was made for. Let Your healing and comfort flow within me. Let the reality of Your perfect presence be greater than my grief. And let me know the intimate friendship of the Holy Spirit, my ever-present Abba.

CHAPTER THREE

I Am Compassion

"Sing for joy, O heavens! Rejoice, O earth! Burst into song, O mountains! For the Lord has comforted His people and will have compassion on them in their suffering."

Isaiah 49:13, NLT

"Compassion is sometimes the fatal capacity for feeling what it is like to live inside somebody else's skin. It is the knowledge that there can never really be any peace and joy for me until there is peace and joy finally for you too."[4]

—Frederick Buechner

od doesn't care about you. This was the accusation that loomed over me in the hospital as I held my lifeless Anna. Goodbye was imminent. As I looked up at Chris in the privacy of our shared pain, I let myself speak what had been simmering all day: *How could a loving God allow this?* Chris told me the truth, but I couldn't hold it: "Kate, the most unfair thing that ever happened was Jesus dying on the cross for our sins." I knew the sentence. I knew it was the Gospel—the good news. But sitting with death in my trembling arms, that truth didn't feel good enough for me.

---

4   Buechner, Frederick. *Wishful Thinking: A Theological ABC.* HarperCollins, 2004, p. 9.

How can God be good amidst pain? This is the question I am most often asked by my suffering friends, who follow Jesus, and those who don't. The valley of pain is where faith often goes to die. It's the hardest question with a holy answer. I loved you *so* much, that I allowed my *only* child to die so that *you* could belong to me always and forever (John 3:16). Compassion is the love and power of Father God that nailed His Son to the cross, surged into the depths of Hell, and resurrected His Son from the tomb. He saw us in the garden. He saw us in the wilderness. He saw us in Galilee and in every corner of the globe. He saw that we were harassed and helpless like sheep without a shepherd, and He came. Compassion lives and breathes in the present risen Jesus who is with us and for us. If we could only peer with the eyes of our spirits, we would see His heart compelled, His love reaching for the wounds and wildness in each of us. The most crucial component of God's love amidst our suffering is His heart of compassion.

On a larger scale, we might *comprehend* compassion—"God loves me, God died for me." But on a personal level, it seems distant and elusive. Like a cloud, we acknowledge it's there, but can't hold it or make it ours. How do we encounter and rely on the compassion we so desperately need?

God's compassion was given weight and substance as I wept on the floor to a recording of Brennan Manning, my junior year of college. Despite my efforts, I have been unable to locate the exact recording, but in his rich, raspy tone, Brennan made the tender empathy of God both accessible and experiential for me. I remember him explaining that the Old Testament word for compassion (*racham*) means a mother's womb, and the New Testament word (*splanchna*) refers to the internal organs, the heart, lungs, liver, and intestines.[5] Both words reveal the place where compassion dwells—the very depths of our being, the places that nurture and sustain life. He explains that compassion is a bursting forth of our inner selves. Compassion isn't just a feeling; it's a physical reaction—an assertive response of holy love reaching empathetically to both comfort and rescue. As Brennan spoke, the cloud that seemed so impossible to me before was now tangible. Almost by instinct, I reached and received the reaching heart of God for me. As I lay there lonely and afraid at the age of twenty, I suddenly felt safe, like I had just been drawn out from consuming waters. I felt cherished like the One who saved me was enraptured by me. To encounter holy compassion is to know that you are both completely saved and desperately loved by the one and only Great I AM. It was compassion that lunged God Almighty from the perfection of heaven and into a burning bush. Remember, Yahweh told Moses He was deeply concerned and therefore responding to the cries of His suffering children. It was compassion that moved Jesus from the magnificence of paradise into the womb of a virgin girl. He came to Mary and told her she would house the Savior and King of Kings within her. Our God was a lifeguard, standing from His throne and diving into the tumultuous waves of the earth to rescue us, urged entirely by the compassionate quality of His perfect love. We don't have to worry or wonder how our God feels when we suffer. He is deeply concerned and moved with compassion.

The story that comforts me most as I search for the heart of God in my sorrow is penned by the beloved disciple John. It's a sacred moment He witnessed in Jesus' ministry—so intimate and rich

---

5 Strong, James. *Strong's Exhaustive Concordance of the Bible*. Thomas Nelson, 1990. Entry H7356, G4698.

in love for those gripped by grief. We see the guttural movement of emotion from His depths expressed as mourning *and* might.

Jesus is approached by His dear friend, Mary of Bethany, who falls at His feet and painfully emotes, "...Lord, if you had been here, my brother would not have died" (John 11:32, ESV).She falls to the ground and weeps at Jesus' feet. When He sees her weeping, the text tells us He was deeply moved and troubled in spirit. He then asks, "Where have you laid him?" Those who accompanied Mary replied, "Come and see" (John 11:32–34, ESV). But before Jesus takes another step, we see His glory expressed in grief: two simple words—a noun and a verb, a name, and an action:

"Jesus wept" (John 11:35, ESV). When Jesus encountered the quake of Mary's deep grief, He was shaken to the core and split open with sorrow Himself. Weeping was the sound that emerged from His broken heart as He felt Mary's pain and His own. In fact, He was so profoundly overcome with grief that onlookers remarked, "...See how he loved him!" (John 11:36, ESV).We don't ever have to wonder how Jesus, the visible image of the invisible God, responds when we suffer. When we weep, He weeps because He loves us. Lament is the language of deepest love flowing as a force of compassion amidst pain. We are deluded to think that God is uninfluenced by, dismissive of, or even dismayed by our feelings. Not only does He feel the sadness we feel, but He also invites our authentic feelings and expresses His own. He is not *far*, but "*near* to the brokenhearted" (Psalm 34:18, ESV; emphasis added). This word in Hebrew for near is *qārôḇ* and infers causality, as in our brokenness draws Him even closer.[6]I am convinced that if the curtain of this realm were pulled back for me to see Jesus the

---

6   Strong, James. *Strong's Exhaustive Concordance of the Bible*. Thomas Nelson, 1990. Entry H7138.

night Anna died, I would've seen Him weeping with and for us. Our doctor and nurses would've had no choice but to remark, "See how He loves them." For years, I looked to this passage in my pain to remind myself that I AM cries with me. But there is another emotion displayed by Jesus that we might miss entirely if we don't look closely enough: "When Jesus saw her weeping, and the Jews who had come with her also weeping, he was deeply moved in his spirit and greatly troubled" (John 11:33, ESV). I always assumed the expression "deeply moved" to be synonymous with Jesus' grief. However, the Greek word for the expression "deeply moved" is *embrimaomai,* which means, sternly to charge; to snort with anger, and to have indignation.[7] The verses go on to say that Jesus was "troubled" (*tarrasso*), meaning to stir or to trouble, as in boiling water.[8] The death of Lazarus simmered within Jesus to a raging boil of indignant anger. Oh, how I wish I had understood all those years ago that righteous indignation was felt by the Holy One in the same way His sorrow was felt. When my daughter died, I trembled with a startling and terrifying anger, pulsing with indignation. I could not unhook myself from the need to blame. I shook my finger at God, and I hated myself for it. But Jesus, in His grief, also surges with anger and points His finger of blame. The difference is who He points at.

Jesus gives us the answer plain and clear in John 10:10 (NIV; emphasis added), "The thief comes *only* to steal, kill, and destroy...". If we can stay here for a moment, we can sit in the cause and the answer to our boiling indignation. We can know where to

---

7   Strong, James. *Strong's Exhaustive Concordance of the Bible.* Thomas Nelson, 1990. Entry G1690.

8   Strong, James. *Strong's Exhaustive Concordance of the Bible.* Thomas Nelson, 1990. Entry G5015.

place our fury. When the enemy strikes us, Jesus is an angry dad. "How dare you hurt my kids!"

I bet you can relate to that feeling. There is a fierce anger that arises when someone we love gets hurt by another. We become "deeply moved" in spirit and "troubled," just like Jesus. The verse goes on to reveal the true character and nature of our Father's heart: "...I came that they may have life and have it abundantly" (John 10:10, NIV). There is no question as to who is at fault when death and destruction mar our lives. There is no question as to God's intentions for us. The enemy is always, and will always be, to blame; Jesus, however, will always be our rescuer and our supplier of abundance. The cruelty of the devil ignites the compassion of God. Jesus told those present to take away the stone, but Martha sought to reason with Him that the odor of death would be too strong. "Jesus said to her, 'Did I not tell you that if you believed you would see the glory of God?'" (John 11:40, ESV). At this announcement, the stone was moved. Jesus prayed aloud to His father and then with a loud voice He cried, "Lazarus, come out" (John 11:43, ESV). The man who had died came out, his hands and feet bound with linen strips, and his face wrapped with a cloth. Jesus said to them, "Unbind him, and let him go" (John 11:44, ESV).

Isn't this a marvel? Isn't this abundant? Jesus, full of gut-wrenching and lunging emotion, displays the sorrow, anger, and power that defines divine compassion. But why did Jesus wait to exercise His power over Lazarus? Why sit in the downpour of grief when He could've skipped the sorrow? Four days before Lazarus died, Mary and Martha sent word to Jesus that "... the one you love is sick.' When he heard this, Jesus said, 'This sickness will not end in death. No, it is for God's glory so that God's Son may be glorified through it'" (John 11:3–4, NIV). The death of Lazarus gave the opportunity for compassion to be demonstrated and glorified, first as shared pain and then as power. This is the stunning intersection of grief and glory. The place where the humanity of Jesus (He feels as we do) and the divinity of Jesus (He acts as we can't) collide together. I AM cries with *us,* and I AM resurrects us. God's allowance for tragedies in our lives doesn't exclude Him from feeling the weight or pain of them. In fact, this is the reason Jesus says to His disciples, "...In this world you will have trouble. But take heart! I have overcome the world" (John 16:33, NIV). In essence, it's as if He is saying, "Until I return for good, you will be caught in the crossfire of the devil's schemes to harm you. He can hurt, but not destroy you. I have already won that war. I have defeated the devil. Comfort is my long game, and resurrection is my endgame. You win in both." This is where we wait on the Lord. We rest in His compassion while waiting for His power. We wish it weren't like this, don't we? We wish there weren't a devil who steals our goods and identities, kills those we love, and destroys what we hold dear. We wish we didn't have to hurt. This is why it is so imperative that we can know and trust God's posture in our pain. Suffering added to His Spirit is like yeast to bread. It causes the compassionate love of God to grow, for the spring within to surge fast and furious, just as His tears flow. We can count on Jesus as a grieved companion *and* as the great commander for the resurrection of our lives. God's power is His righteous checkmate to the enemy's last move. He will always be the victor. We may not be able to see every move on this side of heaven or even understand His process, but we can be certain that He is acting on our behalf. We know our stories through the lens of time, but God sees our lives as unfolding outside of time. In a very real sense, the death of my daughter happened at the same moment Jesus went to the cross. When He rose from the grave, He cursed the devil and took Anna with Him. When He rose from the grave, He redeemed my pain. When He rose from the grave, every moment of my life, burial, and resurrection with Him already took place. When we can't see the fingerprints of God in our daily sorrow, we can look to God's Word, to the past and future record that displays His almighty hands. In every situation we face, we can rest in the truth that God is our compassionate champion.

There is a specific moment in my grief journey, an encounter so unparalleled with the beautiful and powerful compassion of Jesus, that I must share it with you. However, to share this story, I must first tell you about the rest of our children: Just one year after Anna Rose was born still (2005), John Christopher (2006) was born kicking and screaming. Then came Benjamin Kyle (2007), Elijah Andrew (2011), Jonah Davis (2014), and then Vivian Joy Noelle (2017).

When Vivian turned two, we couldn't shake the desire for one final baby. But nine months and three early miscarriages later, we mournfully decided our family was complete. We went on an amazing trip to Europe with our best friends and celebrated all that was behind and before us. We were at peace. But one month later, I began to feel a very familiar type of nausea and fatigue. We were surprised to learn we were pregnant once again.

Nervous days turned into weeks, and my belly began to bulge, and nearly three months passed. I stared at the ultrasound monitor and saw our little love kicking away, arms and legs dancing, and I sank into joy and peace. This sweetheart would make it. I knew it. A day later, we arrived at the doctor's office again to hear my blood test results. I'd prepared myself for some measure of difficult news. Instead, "completely healthy girl" was joyfully spoken. Chris and I found ourselves standing at the top of a mountain. The view was breathtaking. Tears fell as we laughed and embraced. Suffering was past, and a new song could be sung. I had longed for another daughter for years. God answered that prayer in Vivian! But to have two daughters and for Vivi Joy to have a sister was a dream come true. It was as if the Lord took the deepest desire of my heart, the one I was too afraid to utter, and He handed it to me on a golden platter. I could barely contain my joy as I climbed onto the patient table, up to the summit. Joy and laughter leaped from my lips. It was a near song until the scream emerged. Then the monitor revealed a lifeless baby. No beating heart. No dancing limbs. Just a motionless baby girl. For the second time in my life, I looked at Chris in horrified desperation. I demanded breathlessly, "Where is her heartbeat? Where is it?" I begged as if he had the power to give an answer other than *gone*. I knew this man would wrestle sharks and lasso stars for his wife to be spared one more ounce of pain. But there was nothing he could do but grab my hand and plead continuously, "I'm so sorry." I screamed repeatedly, unable to contain my horror. Angels went before us to the hospital. Chris and I held hands and cried until the nurse came to take me away. Chris let go of me and tearfully watched as I was wheeled down the hall. It hurts to even write about it. "Together" was safe. "Alone" was treacherous. I had to endure the hardest part alone. The last thing I remember was apologizing through uncontrollable sobs as I was lifted onto the surgical table. "Please don't let go of my hands," I begged my masked nurses. They squeezed tight, nodding their heads as I drifted to sleep. I woke to the sound of my own sobs and pained proclamations: "My baby, my baby," I wept repeatedly. The nurse rushed to get Chris. I was relieved when my sister Kristen accompanied him into the room. Anesthesia was warring on me. I came and went to the image of Chris weeping, Kristen consoling. Chris went home to comfort our grieving children, and Kristen took me to my parents' house to recover. I climbed into bed and closed my eyes, exhausted from surgery and suffering. Though my body reached for sleep, intrusive thoughts advanced against me—catastrophic scenes of dying children I was paralyzed to rescue. I began screaming in fear and helplessness. I screamed until I felt Kristen's arms tight around me. I heard the pain in her words as she cried out, "Oh Jesus, we need you." Repeatedly, she begged the God of rescue to come near. Her words flung the door of heaven wide open, and this was the moment when the miraculous compassion of God descended upon me. As Kristen beseeched Jesus to comfort and deliver me, the scary images were replaced by the image of my body curled in grief, lying on a stunning white and gray marble floor. I was alone on this luxurious, cold surface, weeping. And then I saw angels—hundreds of them—above me staring in wondrous anticipation as if the sun was about to rise. Then Jesus walked toward me. He knelt over me and wept, His body heaving with the force. He lavished on me a lamenting love. It was as if He was saying, "I am in pain too, and I will handle this." He stroked my hair in sync with my sister's hand. Again, I saw the angel's faces. Their emotion was nearly palpable. They watched in awe at Jesus's compassion for me. The fascination and joyful wonder on their faces boasted that "we" were truly beautiful. My grief and His comfort were glorious to them. I faintly recalled the Scripture, "... Even angels long to look into these things" (1 Peter 1:12, NIV). Mercy and comfort, the crux of God's love, is something the angels could only witness but never experience. I saw my pain in that moment from heaven's viewpoint, the esteemed recipient of His compassionate care. Though I had yelled earlier that day of His cruelty, at this moment, all I wanted was Him closer. I fell asleep to the stroke of the Savior's hand and my sister's that night under a canopy of envious holy beings, mesmerized by the love of the

Father for His grieving child. This experience with compassionate Jesus was the moment I knew I would survive and heal. It was my John 11 moment with Him. From grieving Mary to grieving Kate, "Jesus wept." I was held in the arms of Yahweh. He would be the strength beneath me to bear the weight and the comfort upon me to soothe the pain. He would point His finger of blame at the enemy and exercise His power in my life with authority: "Kate, come out!" Come out of grief and despair. Come out of the pain of disbelief. Come out of accusation and anger. Come out of hopelessness and fear. No evil, pain, or sorrow is more powerful than the power which *is* Jesus Christ. We may be tempted to feel overpowered under the crushing weight of our losses, but there is nothing we will ever lose that won't be redeemed in eternity. This is the truth, and it gives us courage to endure our suffering with hope. Abundance is a present-tense force flowing restoration into our lives now and resurrection into our permanent future with Him. I know my days of suffering are far from gone, but, I also know there is a day in my future when I will be comforted for the last time: "He will wipe away every tear from their eyes, and death shall be no more, neither shall there be mourning, nor crying, nor pain anymore, for the former things have passed away" (Revelation 21:4, ESV).

Comfort will be complete when we can look into the eyes of the Compassionate One and truly experience the power of complete and total resurrection. He will wipe away our tears with His very fingers and welcome us into His forever presence, free from pain. Can you close your eyes for a moment and imagine this final comfort encounter with Jesus? Can you envision your final tear being wiped away by I AM, the One, who is currently grieved, angry, and emitting power on your behalf?

I wish I could sit with each of you to hear your story. I wish you could see the compassion in my eyes for the wounds and wildness in you. And though each of our stories is different, I know we all have the same attacker *and* the same Dad—Father God, Jesus the compassionate one.

In what ways have you been hurt by the thief? What despair has caused you to question God's love and compassion toward you?

I want to extend the invitation for you to open the eyes of your heart to the Savior who has dropped to the ground to join you in your grief. To believe that the rage you may feel is only a fraction of the anger He feels toward your shared enemy. To know that today, right now, as you read, a force of the greatest love and power is already working resurrection into your life.

Compassionate I AM, the One who suffers with and for me, the One who holds both ache and anger for the sin, death, and despair that seek to consume. Open the eyes of my heart to see Your knees on the dirt of my darkest soil and the tears You weep because You love me. Thank you that the sound of my pain draws You even nearer to me. Fill me with the truth that there is nothing that could ever separate me from Your love. Thank You for the ways You have already determined to redeem—even though I can't see them now. Help me to trust in Your resurrection plan for all the pain in my life. Give me the gift of knowing You intimately and the healing that flows from abiding in, loving, and depending on You, my ever-present I AM.

CHAPTER FOUR

I Am Rest

"Come to me, all you who labor and are heavy laden, and I will give you rest."

Matthew 11:28, ESV

"You have made us for yourself, O Lord, and our hearts are restless until they rest in You."[9]

—Saint Augustine

I never took naps until I got married. The rising and setting of the sun dictated my pace. Daytime was for accomplishing, and nighttime was for sleeping. What could a nap possibly accomplish? To me, a daytime pause was a waste of life. But then, I fell in love with a napper. Since my husband is the most amazing person in my world, I was forced to rethink my napping theory. Though the hobby seemed ridiculous to me, out of a desire to be with Chris, I joined him one Sunday afternoon. At first, I lay there restless, wishing the time would pass quickly so I could get up. My mind raced. How was I supposed to sleep in a sunlit room when I wasn't tired? How could he fall asleep so easily? But then I settled in and eventually smiled as purpose came into focus. This was being,

---

9   Augustine of Hippo. *The Confessions of Saint Augustine*. Translated by Edward B Pusey, Peter Pauper Press, 1945. Book 1, Chapter 1, p. 1.

not doing, and this was companionship with the safest person in my world. My husband's unhurried and steady nature was inviting me to something much deeper than a nap.

An hour later, I woke up next to my beloved and felt the most incredible calm. It wasn't the rest that gave me that, but rather the one I was resting with. I could cease striving when I was lying with the one who loved me for me. A sobering reflection dawned. Were my busyness and helpfulness motivated by the fear of worthlessness? Napping meant I had to trust that my inactivity wasn't costing me. To truly rest, I had to lay down my tools of performance and advancement. I had to be okay with imperfection. I had to… surrender. Only blankets of thickest grace could enable this rest. Chris was good at using these blankets. His easy-going personality made napping desirable, and his profession as a pastor made Sabbath rest essential. Lying down to pause was a physical, emotional, and spiritual need he surrendered to. I had so much to learn from the man I loved. Being forgiven infinitely and loved unconditionally were beds I loved to make, but struggled to lie in. Unfortunately, our Sunday afternoon rhythm quickly faded when life got fuller and busier, and sabbath afternoons weren't just for the two of us. Year after year, child after child, naptime was replaced with laundry to fold, toilets to clean, meals to cook, and a week ahead to plan. Life got harder, too. I started to feel like a break for me meant a break somewhere else. I stayed busy in order to keep us whole, but then life turned fragile. Our world turned upside down, and every wall, floor, and child seemed to be made of glass. Rest wasn't an option when there were so many things and people to keep from shattering. When the earth beneath us began to shake, no matter how hard I mothered and loved, I couldn't keep the walls from crashing down. Finally, there was a total collapse, a complete undoing… and it was me.

When Elijah was four, we knew something was different, but we couldn't put our finger on it. After a few doctor's visits and appointments with audiologists, he was diagnosed with Auditory Processing Disorder. Two years later, he was diagnosed with significant anxiety. The year after that, several unspecified learning disabilities. The following year, ADHD, and at age nine, he was diagnosed with Autism. Such a dear boy was dealt such a difficult hand. Elijah was tormented by his own inabilities and insecurities in a world that isn't made for those with social, language, and sensory disorders. He couldn't find words to understand or communicate his frustrations, discomforts, and needs. All he had was overwhelm, excessive tears, and extreme behaviors to match.

We loved and parented the way we always had, and yet we seemed to fail at every turn. We sought pediatric neurologists, psychologists, psychiatrists, geneticists, naturopathic doctors, and various other therapists to give answers, direction, and hope. Our other four children were sad and scared. The older boys isolated themselves in their rooms while the youngest two panicked and hid when aggressive meltdowns began. A suffering storm raged in our home, and it had a name. How could I love and support Elijah, whose suffering was so remarkably strong, while simultaneously calming and reassuring our other four children? On the first anniversary of the loss of Violet, enduring both grief and the daily stress of living with an autistic child, I had a panic attack that didn't stop. After twenty-four hours of what I can only describe as terror-filled thoughts and images, hyperventilating, and sobbing, I was taken to the emergency room. A terrified Chris stayed with the children, and my sister once again held me in a hospital bed. At first, I was comforted by her presence, but then a stabbing thought emerged as she hovered above me, seeking to console: *Was she going to hurt me?* I wept those words aloud, along with other intrusive thoughts and the very real longing to fall asleep and not wake up. My world had been rocked, and nothing felt trustworthy or safe. In desperation and devastation, I wanted death. I was taken to the psychiatric unit, where I was admitted for a week. I was afraid and ashamed, but also relieved, because for me, home was unsafe. It was the place of all my failures.

The admitting nurse came to take my vitals and asked what felt like a thousand jagged questions. I gave answers the best I could through humiliated sobs. I told her what I could: who I was and how I'd gotten there, but I was so shocked and confused. Was this really happening to me? Was I really failing as a wife and mother to my family? As an answer to my pained bewilderment, she said, "I know why you're here."

I stared and she continued:

"This is your Holy Pause. God is giving you a safe space to rest and receive what you need from Him and from us. You've been lighting yourself on fire to keep everyone else warm. You can't do that and not end up here. You need to rest and learn how to take care of yourself. You need to breathe."

Her words blessed and broke me. She was right. I was charred to a crisp from years of heating our home with my very life, but I didn't know another way. I had never felt more like a failure, never more pathetic or worthless than this very moment. She placed a very small, very strong pill in my hand and told me it would give my brain and body rest. The first three days, all I did was weep and sleep. I was catching up on both. By the fourth day, I had finally purged enough tears and slept enough hours that I could hold a conversation. I welcomed the hospital chaplain that afternoon.

"Kate, have you heard of Lectio Divina?" She explained that it was a divine monastic practice of Scripture reading intended to promote communion with God. She asked if I had a favorite passage. I asked her to choose her favorite for me. She encouraged me to picture myself in the story, to let the Spirit speak to and guide me. I was ready to receive whatever I could from the Lord. She opened her Bible and read:

> Then he got into the boat and his disciples followed him. Suddenly a furious storm came up on the lake, so that the waves swept over the boat. But Jesus was sleeping. The disciples went and woke him, saying, 'Lord, save us! We're going to drown!' He replied, 'You of little faith, why are you so afraid?' Then he got up and rebuked the winds and the waves, and it was completely calm. The men were amazed and asked, 'What kind of man is this? Even the winds and the waves obey him!' (Matthew 8:23–27, NIV)

Her voice was melodic. The verses were a near lullaby on her lips, and I felt rocked by the words.

By the end of the third reading, I was fully curled up with Jesus on the boat. I could nearly smell the salty air and hear the creak of wooden boards moved by turbulent water beneath me. I was able to *feel* myself in the story. I was safe in the arms of Almighty Jesus, and His peace enveloped me. It was the first time I'd *felt* peace in months. I began to cry because this beautiful encounter wasn't the reality of my life experience, and I didn't know how not to be afraid within my unrelenting, raging reality. *Don't you care that we are going to drown? Wake up, Jesus! Do something, please?* I was frantically trying to scoop water out of the boat to keep from drowning when what I really needed to do was curl up with the only One who could save me. My dear nurse, Kara, was also present in the room. With tenderness in her eyes and her voice, she spoke, "Kate, I keep hearing, 'you are not alone.' I'll say it again and again: you are not alone. You are not alone. You are not alone." Her words dug deeper and deeper within me until they were underneath me, like cradling arms.

The chaplain began to sing a hymn, which I felt certain she had sung to many others on this floor before. Her voice lulled me into a deep place of want. I wanted to be okay when nothing was okay. I wanted to know how to cease striving, to be still, and to know that He was God (Psalm 46:10, NIV). As I closed my eyes, and my hospital bed became the floor of the boat, once again I was wrapped in I AM, and her voice carried on the wind:

> Jesus, I am resting, resting
> In the joy of what Thou art;
> I am finding out the greatness
> of Thy loving heart.
> Thou hast bid me gaze upon Thee,
> As thy beauty fills my soul,
> for by Thy transforming power,
> Thou hast made me whole.[10]

I was the opposite of whole. I was pieces and fragments, but beginning to understand that the path before me was one to wholeness. I couldn't muster a single word, but my spirit responded to the invitation that kept repeating in my mind, "...Come to me, all you who are weary and burdened, and I will give you rest. Take my yoke upon you, and learn from me, for I am gentle and lowly in heart, and you will find rest for your souls..." (Matthew 11:28–30, ESV). I wanted to rest with Jesus. I wanted the safety, security, and soul peace of resting with I AM. I just didn't know how.

---

10 Pigott, Jean Sophia. *Jesus, I Am Resting, Resting.* 1877.

Later that afternoon, I picked up a book Chris had brought to me. Just a few pages in, I realized I was holding one of those books that would change my life forever. In the first chapter of *Gentle and Lowly*, Dane Ortlund shares his thoughts regarding the "Come to Me" verse:

> In the one place in the Bible where the Son of God pulls back the veil and lets us peer way down into the core of who He is, we are not told that He is 'austere and demanding in heart.' We are not told that He is 'exalted and dignified in heart.' We are not even told that He is 'joyful and generous in heart.' Letting Jesus set the terms, His surprising claim is that He is gentle and lowly in heart... Jesus is not trigger happy. Not harsh, reactionary or easily exasperated. He is the most understanding person in the universe. The posture most natural to Him is not a pointed finger but open arms.[11]

I read and reread these words. I was stunned. The author just rearranged God's personality, and I didn't quite know what to do with it. He revealed a God whose love emanated first through gentleness and approachable humility. Of course, I knew these were characteristics of Jesus, but they didn't feel like the most prominent qualities of Him. To process and understand that "gentle and lowly" were the characteristics Jesus would use to describe Himself shook me to the core. Could I really believe that the two qualities most prevalent in God's heart toward me were gentle and lowly? Not irritated and impatient? Not embarrassed and ashamed? Not even perfect and powerful. Jesus offered me Himself as gentle and lowly

---

11 Ortlund, Dane. *Gentle and Lowly: The Heart of Christ for Sinners and Sufferers*. Crossway, 2020, p. 18.

(approachable). I was struggling to believe this to be true. The tears fell as I wrestled. That's when the whisper emerged: "Kate." It was easy to dismiss amid the heaving of my grief. But then the voice from within softly beckoned again: "Baby Doll."

Something inside me settled and woke simultaneously. These were my mama's words for me, tender words that made me feel small and held, even at forty-two. Was she here? Of course, I knew she wasn't, but the presence that came with the whisper was so strong, I had to look around the room. I lay back down, somewhat comforted and somewhat scared. I'd asked the nurses to keep my door locked so I wouldn't have to fear wandering patients. As I lay back down on my pillow, the fear dissipated as revelation descended. Jesus used the sweet and nurturing words of my mother, the most gentle and lowly person I've ever known, to introduce me to *Him*. Of course, Mama was gentle because *He* was gentle first and always.

I could nearly feel His breath upon me. A confident calm fell over me, a blanket of plush peace. I was speechless. I lay completely still. I wanted nothing to disrupt this miraculous moment. Did Jesus really long to nurture and comfort me like my mother? Would he really and truly call me "Baby Doll," the same words I now use to beckon my babies to reassurance, belonging, and love? The answer is a resounding "yes," and I love the way I AM assures me of this in Isaiah 62:2 (ESV): "You shall be called by a new name that the mouth of the Lord will give. You shall be called 'My Delight Is in Her.'"

This new understanding of Jesus' nature and His perfect, tender love for me began casting out my fear (1 John 4:18). God wasn't disappointed in me. I belonged to Him, and He *delighted* in me because I was His. I *could* relax. I *could* rest, because I no longer needed to be afraid of my failures or an impatient, irritable God. Jesus wasn't upset with me. He wanted me to know, believe, and rest within the truth: that I am His child and He is my caretaker.

When the disciples cried out in fear of being drowned, they didn't know or believe the complete truth of the God that was with them. When Jesus calmed the storm, they were shocked. "Who is this *man?*" they essentially asked. Though they believed Jesus enough to follow Him, their hearts were not yet convinced of His power and His provision (Mark 4:35–41; emphasis added). They didn't know Him yet as their Savior. That came after the resurrection. That's when they all risked their lives and charged into storms, ready to die for their Master *and* Messiah.

Here we are now, thousands of years later, with the gift of salvation and the Holy Spirit of God to testify to our souls. This is our great privilege. This is what made my tears fall repeatedly as I rested in that hospital bed for several more days. I wasn't safe because of the absence of the storm, I was safe because of the gentle and *great* God who was present in it. After seven days of holy pausing, I was discharged from the hospital. My dear Chris picked me up and took me away for a night to rest before returning home. The only available place he could find was a newly renovated hotel, which had once been a psychiatric hospital—the scary kind. It sat abandoned for decades with wire coils wrapped around tall fences and broken windows everywhere. The irony was stunning; we were leaving one hospital and checking into another. This place, once an institution of unrest for the unwilling, was now a haven of deepest rest for me. I wanted all the restoration and renovation I could get. This hotel, situated on a hill with acres of lush, green, weeping cherries and a river winding through, was the setting of my Twenty-Third Psalm. These were my green pastures and quiet waters to restore my soul. It was a physical place and a spiritual picture of what my Deliverer was doing for me and in me.

I reentered my life with no answers as to how to rescue our children, but I held a permanent invitation to rest with the One who could. The most essential thing I could do for our children was to model desperation and dependence. They had to see and believe that Mama trusted in almighty Jesus, even as our boat was tossed to and fro. This wasn't (and isn't) easy. It wasn't instinctual. This was faith and the hardest trust I'd ever fought for. I would have to learn to recline with Jesus and fight against my human urge to figure it all out, fix things, and be our family savior. I would have to repeatedly pull back the blankets and climb into His invitation to "come and rest" and to "be still and know that He is God."

Within the next several months, I received even greater information about how much rest was needed. A new doctor and new blood work revealed thyroid disease, severe anemia, vitamin deficiency, hormone imbalance, and adrenal failure. The battle I'd been fighting wasn't just circumstantial but also physical. My doctor was shocked that I hadn't crashed sooner with such a failing engine. New prescriptions were given for how to heal. My doctor gave me new supplements, vitamins, hormones, medications, iron infusions, and a prescription for months of sleep. Rest wasn't just a suggestion, it was a requirement. This meant I would have to learn to surrender everything. I agreed not to say "yes" to anything without processing it with Chris. He helped me to uncover what was behind my yes. Was it a have-to or a want-to? Was it feeding into unnecessary striving or aiding my rest? I surrendered to let my sisters, Kristen and Melissa, determine and plan how to provide the practical help we needed. Babysitters were hired to care for the kids and do the laundry. Dear friends provided food, cleaning, and support in so many ways. Help kept coming, and in humility, I learned to receive it. As I surrendered, slept, and stayed consistent with therapy and doctor's appointments, I slowly began to heal. Eventually, God began rebuking the winds and the waves in our world, but first He rebuked the winds and waves within me. "Peace be still" to my fears, to my false beliefs about God, my unhealthy and unhelpful rhythms and defenses, my legalism and religiosity, my disappointment and grief. "Peace be still" to me. I had to learn to stop and to breathe... literally.

My therapist, Dana, was the one who first taught me the importance of breathwork. Deep breathing isn't simply a relaxation strategy; it's a simple brain *reforming* strategy. For me, this intentional rhythm felt unmeaningful at first, but I quickly learned its power for the body. It's a way to intercept feelings and affect change in the brain. When combined with prayer, change also erupts in the soul, too. No one explains this better than Jennifer Tucker in her book, *Breath as Prayer,* a book that now sits in a treasured stack with my Bible:

> Breath prayers combine two powerful tools that can help calm anxiety: the science of deep breathing and the prayers of meditation on God's word... Breath prayers are short, mostly one sentence prayers, rooted in scripture and aligned with the rhythm of the breath. The first half is prayed while inhaling, the second half is prayed while exhaling and repeated several times for the purpose of meditating on God's word. As you practice breath prayers, you begin to change the neural networks in your brain. In science they call this neuroplasticity: your brain is a dynamic organ that can change and be shaped

as you learn and grow and experience new things. I like to think of it as a remarkable example of how you are literally being transformed by the renewing of your mind (Romans 12:2).[12]

Praying on breath in this way has dramatically impacted my healing. Using breath prayer in conjunction with Scripture visualization has been transformative. For example, in visualizing myself stepping into the boat with Jesus and resting with Him as my storm of anxiety or fear rages, I inhale, "Peace," and exhale, "Be still." I breathe in grace and release pain. I inhale love and exhale fear. I inhale Jesus and exhale… me. It's a spiritual and physiological avenue to real change that can be believed and felt. As I write today, nearly five years have passed since my "holy pause," and I am resting on the boat, breathing deep with Jesus still. This posture is not because I have reached some superhuman level where the waves no longer terrify me. It's not that I've reached a level of holiness that I can override my natural instinct to fear. Resting with Jesus is still and will always be about surrendering and knowing. It's not a one-time sacrifice or realization. It's a relationship. It's a continual experience. It is ongoing, and a precious intimacy with the Almighty.

In my growth as a disciple of Jesus, an apprentice of courage, I will never graduate from being His child. This is the "I am" that anchors and defines me most clearly: "I am a child of God." I am His "baby doll" first and foremost. I will never reach a stage of maturity where I need Him less. Perhaps the more "adult" I become, the more I understand His words: "Truly, I say to you, unless you change and become like little children, you will never enter the

---

12 Tucker, Jennifer. *Breath as Prayer: Calm Your Anxiety, Focus Your Mind, and Renew Your Soul*. Thomas Nelson, 2022. p. 17.

kingdom of heaven" (Matthew 18:3, ESV). The day God called me "baby doll" was the day He spoke these words to me personally: "Kate, become a child once again and enter the kingdom of abundance I have for you, here and now."

As life swells, crests, and crashes into our boat, I can now crawl more confidently, a desperate child across the floors of unwanted circumstance. I fall helpless—but not hopeless—into the arms of Jesus. As I learn to define Him, He grandeurs from "this man" to "*my* God." Sometimes it's a simple perspective shift that takes a few moments, and feelings of calm follow. But more often than not, this "resting" is a whole season of remembering (breathing) and defining how good, glorious, great, and gracious God truly is. It's in the practice of "knowing him" that my body, mind, and spirit can align with and agree that I am ultimately enveloped in the arms of my Savior, not the claws of the storm. It's in this intentional remembrance of the one who declares me "baby doll" that I can rest safely amidst the storm.

Every Sunday, we nap. Chris preaches, and then we come home and collapse into rest. We accept the invitation to sabbath, to make the seventh day our "holy pause." From the first pages of Scripture, God commands rest as a need and an answer. Man toiled and strived until a permanent Sabbath was born—Jesus. That perfect rest grew, loved, taught, healed, performed miracles, calmed storms, died, and rose again. He became the definition of weary and heavy-laden so we could be free. He triumphed once and for all in the ways we could not and by doing so, extended the victorious invitation to deepest rest; everyday sabbath from everyday grace. This rest is the effect of knowing Jesus.

I am so grateful that I now look confidently to the God who is my Daddy—a God of tenderness who rocks me to sleep in holy grace. His promises cause me a deep sigh of relief and a song of praise: "For I will satisfy the weary soul, and every languishing soul I will replenish" (Jeremiah 31:25, ESV). I AM says "I will" to the stormy soul. I AM says "Peace, be still" to our winds and waves. I AM says, "Come unto me, and rest."

The boat rocks. Grey skies cry, and tears follow. My spirit yawns, and the covers of grace are pulled high. Weariness recedes as worship ascends. This is precious grace, and it is gifted to me from the Savior of souls and storms. He *is* gentle and lowly, and I am His.

Weary friend, how is it for you? Soul exhaustion is a reality we will experience again and again as we run, walk, and crawl through our sorrows. We can't escape the storms. We can't unwrite the hospitals, deaths, abuse, and brokenness that life will spell out for us. But we also can't erase God's Word, and He tells us truthfully, tenderly, and repeatedly:

"...Fear not, for I have redeemed you; I have called you by name, you are mine" (Isaiah 43:1, ESV).

"Behold, I have engraved you on the palms of my hands; your walls are continually before me" (Isaiah 49:16, ESV).

"...The Lord called me from the womb, from the body of my mother he named my name" (Isaiah 49:1, ESV).

And finally...

"...To the one who conquers, I will give some of the hidden manna, and I will give him a white stone, with a new name written on the stone that no one knows except the one who receives it" (Revelation 2:17, ESV).

Friend, today as you turn these pages, as you trudge through the hard and weep in the sadness, the name given to you by Jesus is being softly spoken over you. Your ability to hear it does not change the truth that a very powerful and intimate God is beckoning you to Himself. He invites you to a miraculous and deep soul rest, even within restless waves. We can be calm conquerors as we trust the One who commands that which rages in our lives. On the day when perfect and complete rest is given to us, we will receive a stone with the name He whispered to us all our lives. Faith will become sight—a seeing, hearing, and knowing reality. But until then… "Come unto me, *beloved*, and rest."

God of Rest, I need You. I am weary and worn out from unrelenting winds and waves. I am exhausted from the burdens in my life and in relationships. I am sick of the lies that won't let me go. I need to know Your gentle and lowly heart. I need to know that You delight in me. I am desperate for the space in Your arms where all is safe when nothing feels safe. I am aching to be whole amidst all that is broken. Hear my cry: "I don't know what to do, but my eyes are on you" (2 Chronicles 20:12, NIV). *I look to You, Savior of the sabbath, and lean into You, the One who calms my storms. Thank You for naming me and calling me by name. Let my spirit be quieted by Your intimate whisper, which is always beckoning me. Flood me now with the peace that comes from surrender and give me the rest I long for.*

CHAPTER FIVE

I Am Faithful

"Lord, you are my God; I will exalt you and praise your name, for in perfect faithfulness you have done wonderful things, things planned long ago."

Isaiah 25:1, NIV

"Thanksgiving for God's faithfulness in our pain is the indisputable proof that we believe God is a part of our pain."[13]

—Erwin W. Lutzer

I looked up and all around me. I was the youngest person in our Sloop family circle. All nineteen of us held hands in the small kitchen at Mission Haven. The memory seems like an old photograph on a special page in the book of that year, colors faded yet still warm. The Martins (my dad's sister's family) had returned from Brazil on furlough. I had missed them so much. We gathered to welcome them at Columbia Seminary's missionary housing in Decatur, Georgia, and to celebrate Thanksgiving. We were all eager to eat, but Grandaddy was eager to give thanks. This meant my hunger would grow for at least another ten to fifteen minutes. There was no quick "grace" in this family. Grandaddy said "Amen," and then our sing-along began.

---

13 Lutzer, Erwin W. *When You've Been Wronged: Moving from Bitterness to Forgiveness*. Moody Publishers, 2007, p.63.

Strong voices quickly followed, and harmonies fanned out from the melody. The Sloop quartet, my dad and his three siblings, all knew their parts, and as the rest of us joined in, a choir was born: "*There is no shadow of turning with Thee; Thou changest* not, Thy compassions, they fail not. As Thou hast been, Thou forever will *be.*"

Grandaddy's shiny bald head and rosy cheeks were draped by puffs of cotton hair. His woolly white beard warmed his face, which always looked cold, allowing his generous smile to peek through. Grandaddy was both commanding and cute. His mouth opened wide as he sang, pride and joy for his God leapt from his soul onto every note. He conducted as we sang, "*Great is Thy faithfulness! Great is Thy faithfulness! Morning by morning new mercies I see; All I have needed Thy hand hath provided—Great is Thy faithfulness, Lord, unto me.*"[14]

As the fourth and final verse concluded, my tummy rumbled, and my mouth watered. But then, Grandaddy started to sing the hymn all over again, this time in Portuguese. For forty years, he had spoken this language as a missionary in Brazil. Now all I could do was stare. This wasn't just a song. This was his anthem in a language he learned for a people he loved. He believed every verse and lived his life upon them. Conducting us now was the greatest gift he could possibly give his family. He was *our* missionary, and to Grandaddy, this *was* the meal.

I was thirteen when grandaddy died.

It was the first time I truly grieved. Daddy came in to tell me, and I wept in my sturdy oak chair at my sturdy oak desk. Nothing felt sturdy now. The tears kept coming. It wasn't just because I

---

14   Chisholm, Thomas O. *Great Is Thy Faithfulness*. 1923.

loved him; it was because I *knew* how much he loved me. I expected and craved his delight in me, *his* Katherine, and I was sick with sorrow that I would never feel that from him again. We sang *Great is Thy Faithfulness* at the funeral, though I could barely muster a note through the thick grief in my throat. We continued to sing it over the years at family reunions and weddings. We sang it at Anna's funeral, too. I could almost see Grandaddy conducting and coaching me with his grand smile from the balconies of heaven; "This is it, Katie. This is your moment. This is the day the song becomes *your* anthem." It was the hour to declare what I held to be most true, no matter what happened to me. I clutched Chris's hand, very aware of our audience. Everyone was watching us. My faith was on display. I sang every word, though my soul throbbed with the searing pain of doubt. I wanted it to be true. I wanted to sing with the pride and conviction Grandaddy taught me to sing with. But I wept every note, hoping no one could see. I clung to the faithfulness of God by a thread.

Two weeks passed after the funeral for Anna, and I lay on my bed in agony. My breasts stung from the cruel bite of mastitis, and my body shook with fever. My womb ached from the pain of contractions, and my tailbone throbbed from reinjury during birth. I had every awful symptom to show of new motherhood, and yet no sweet baby to ease my suffering. I had never known such suffocating, unrelenting pain. The misery felt like a disease I would surely die from. I didn't understand why God allowed my baby to die, but certainly He could've been faithful enough to prevent a breast infection? I was drowning in both my woes and whys. I couldn't go on like this anymore. Lying face down, I held my breath and wished for death so I could be with my baby again and leave this grief-stricken body and soul behind. But death didn't come, only the awareness that I was stuck in a life I no longer knew how to live.

Chris came to bring me the mail. I saw *her* handwriting and I tossed everything else aside. My dearest, lifelong friend, Kristin—Krissy. Just holding the letter brought an eruption of tears. She was my kindred spirit. States separated us, but in this dire moment, her words were her voice. She was with me on my bed, she held me and whispered:

"Remember the affliction and my wanderings, the wormwood and the gall. My 'soul continually remembers it and is bowed down within me. But this I call to mind and therefore I have hope: The steadfast love of the Lord never ceases, his mercies never come to an end; they are new every morning, great is your faithfulness. The Lord is my portion, says my soul, therefore I will hope in him! The Lord is good to those who wait on him, to the soul who seeks him. It is good that one should wait quietly for the salvation of the Lord..."

Lamentations 3:19–29

Always,
Kristin

Kristin borrowed Jeremiah's confession of trust in his deepest anguish. She knew me so well. She knew, though I hadn't said a word, that I was wrestling with the faithfulness of God. She knew I felt utterly consumed by sorrow. She knew I would need to be reminded and encouraged to keep believing. Jeremiah understood suffering. His soul was cast down. But with two words, a small and sacred shift, he tilts his soul upward.

"*Yet this.*" Jeremiah forces himself to push lament aside in order to gather memories of God's goodness. He remembers his ancestors, wilderness wanderers, and how they collected manna mercies, morning by morning. Krissy offered Jeremiah as my wilderness guide and urged me to remember. First, she validated my downcast soul, and then she invited me to the bridge of "yet this"—the connector between pain and hope. She was inviting me to recall the faithfulness of God.

Clutching Krissy's words to my chest, I remembered the funeral two weeks before, how I sang this very Scripture, my hymn, as doubt warred against my soul. I was still utterly stabbed with grief, but upon reading and hearing Krissy's words, upon feeling her love for me and our God, I was given a deep breath and a small handful of courage. I wanted to reach for His hand. I wanted the war against Him to cease. I wanted to stop doubting my *Dad*. To confess Him in this moment as faithful meant I would have to acknowledge and accept His permission over the death of my baby and still call Him good. The Hebrew word for faithfulness is munâh, which means firmness, security, and steadiness.[15] The first time munâh appears in the Bible, it describes a supportive measure by Aaron and Hur to Moses in the wilderness. A battle raged against the Israelites. Moses told Joshua to choose men to fight, and that the next day he would stand on the top of the hill with the staff of God in his hand. Whenever Moses held up his hand, Israel succeeded, but whenever he lowered his hand, the enemy prevailed. "But Moses' hands grew weary, so they took a stone and put it under him, and

---

15 Strong, James. *Strong's Exhaustive Concordance of the Bible*. Thomas Nelson, 1990. Entry H530.

he sat on it. Aaron and 'Hur held up his hands, one on one side, and the other on the other side. So, his hands were *steady* (munâh) until the going down of the sun. And Joshua overwhelmed Amalek and his people with the sword" (Exodus 17:12–13, ESV; emphasis added). God knew what Moses was capable of. He knew he couldn't be successful in his own strength. God didn't give Moses a flawed strategy. He gave him one that required munâh—the steadying and faithful support of another. Understanding munâh is the beginning of our deep understanding of God's faithfulness. Our weakness and dependence invite His strong arms underneath our collapsing spirits and doubting songs. God's faithfulness and our victory is most displayed in our desperation and dependence.

Krissy didn't know she was doing it, but when she gave me Lamentations 3:17–20, she set me on a rock and came up under my weak faith with her own strong hands and held me steady. It was my great need that made Krissy's love all the more precious. Kristin was faithful, and she encouraged me to trust in the God whose faithfulness reached right through the timeline of my life—a life for which she had always been present. The root word for 'ĕ-munâh is âman, which means to build up or support; to place a newborn child in the right arm of a father or nurse.[16]How beautiful is this! God's faithfulness is the strong, secure right arm of a father, ready and waiting to support a newborn infant. God is our eager Daddy, arms outstretched to receive, cradle, and support our humanness. Our weakness is the active ingredient, the yeast to His faithfulness. Does the father wait begrudgingly to hold his newborn baby, wailing helplessly in an unfamiliar world? No! It is

---

16 Strong, James. *Strong's Exhaustive Concordance of the Bible.* Thomas Nelson, 1990. Entry H540.

a heart bursting with pride and desire that compels him to reach for His helpless baby.

To know and trust in God's arms, we have to become seekers and finders of all His handprints in our life stories. I have a list that stays tucked in a sacred corner of my heart, a record of faithfulness that starts before I was born. It begins with the womb God faithfully chose as my first home. It continues throughout my life and into the darkest season of grief in 2005:

- He was faithful to provide Krissy's letter as a life preserver when I almost drowned.
- He was faithful to give me a husband who would calm and steady me within my grief and teach me to trust and abide in Christ.
- He was faithful to provide us a new home to rent when we could no longer live in the house of our grief.

Everyday manna. We were being provided for. Those early grieving years are their own chapters, their own records of God's kindness and presence within the meanness of grief. I am so grateful to have such detailed chapters to recall and recite God's faithfulness when we were a grieving family of two. They are manna still for us in the wilderness as a struggling family of seven.

The chapters regarding our wilderness years with Elijah are still being beautifully written. One of the earliest handprints of God pressed into our story was a summer morning in 2020, when tears were the only kind of prayer I could pray. On my knees in desperation, I knelt by Elijah's bed and the Spirit spoke to my heart: "I will make a way where there seems to be no way." I remembered the Exodus, when Moses led his people out of Egypt and to the Red Sea, which at first appeared to be a dead sea. But as Moses raised his right arm in trust and dependence upon, a way appeared.

As I wept for the suffering of my little boy and therefore the suffering for us all, I clung to this miracle and this fresh promise of God's completeness and faithfulness for us. Instantly, I was filled with peace because I knew the Lord would stretch out His arm for us. For nearly a year, this was my prayer on repeat: "You will make a way. You are Yahweh." Our Red Sea parted when we were joined by doctors who understood, medications that helped, therapists who bonded, respite caregivers who sacrificed, community funds distributed, church family and friends who prayed, and a therapy dog that loved. Where there used to be mostly screams, there are now words. Where there used to be rigidity and anger, there is growing flexibility. Where there used to be unhealthy dependence on me, there is now greater independence and reliance on others who love him. Where there used to be stares, there are now smiles, laughs, and jokes. Elijah is beautiful. And so are our other four children, whose wilderness steps have been hard and long. Their wells have been dug deep in grief, anger, and fear. Those wells are filled with manna. Autism is a unique and beautiful ink that is writing all of our stories with dependence and the faithfulness of God.

How exactly do you begin to take steps on the "yet this" bridge to hope? By naming the good things, the smallest crumbs of manna. It's when we recite, "Every good and perfect gift comes from the Father of heavenly lights" (James 1:17, NIV) that the path before us is illuminated.

> A cup of coffee and a quiet moment.
>
> A brave bird on the back porch.
>
> A hot shower and a clean white towel.
>
> An unexpected afternoon nap.
>
> As gratitude rises, awareness broadens, and the manna grows bigger.

A tender look from Chris.

A kiss from Vivian just because.

A Crayola masterpiece from Jonah.

A sympathetic hug and note from Ben.

An honest conversation with John.

The twinkle I almost missed in Elijah's eye.

When I was still waiting for "the way" to appear, remembering who I was in Christ became needed manna, full of the most essential nutrients of faith:

Forgiven and redeemed every single day.

Loved beyond measure every single day.

Seated in heavenly places every single day. Every gift of goodness remembered, every moment of identity recited, and every promise of God repeated is a "yet this" step to hope. How do we know He is faithful? Because He was faithful unto death for the joy set before Him... the joy that is holding you and me. Yes, for the Lord's great love we are not consumed!

I love my morning coffee. In fact, there comes a moment every night when I get excited just thinking about that first hot sip the next morning. I wake up to the smell of dark grounds brewing, and as I select my mug and pour my first cup, I look at the framed picture beside the coffee pot. It's there for a reason; it speaks to me daily of morning mercies. It's a hymn, *our* hymn, and it sings to me:

Great is Thy Faithfulness, O God my Father,

There is no shadow of turning with Thee;

Thou changest not, Thy compassions, they fail not,

As Thou hast been, Thou forever wilt be.

Great is Thy faithfulness! Great is Thy faithfulness!
Morning by morning new mercies I see;
All I have needed Thy hand hath provided—
Great is Thy faithfulness, Lord, unto me

I smile as I take my first sip, and I can almost hear Granddaddy singing from the balconies of heaven. Are my girls by his side? Has he taught them the harmonies? Portuguese? That thought makes me laugh and smile, and I feel His smile upon me, too.

I take my coffee and sit down in my big yellow leather chair in the corner of the sunroom and flip on the fire, the one that makes me warm before there is yet warmth. It reminds me of Yahweh. I look at another framed picture next to my Bible. It's my letter from Krissy from nineteen years ago. It's Lamentations 3 in the handwriting of one of the most beautiful women I've ever known. The Scripture is her arms holding me up, somehow holding me still. This reminds me that I am held in the crook of His right arm, the arm that gives manna and parts seas. The arm that provides doctors, therapists, willing college students, and big fluffy dogs. The God who was with me as I screamed at the deaths of my girls and was with me when newborn babies screamed for life. He is the God who stands at the right hand of His Father's throne and prays without ceasing for me, His nail-scarred hands stretched wide over the timeline of all my days. This is the never-departing, never-giving-up, never ceasing God who delights to save us and steady us with Himself. He is our strong tower. No wind can tear Him down, and no demon can back Him away. He is before us, within us, and beyond us. Yes, I AM has always been faithful to me.

How do you feel about your Father's arms? Are there circumstances and seasons so devastating that you believe He dropped or rejected you? It's important to pause here and to reflect upon the agonized cry of our Savior from the cross: "...My God, my God, why have you forsaken me?" (Matthew 27:46, ESV). It is both human and holy to direct our pained questions to the Lord. With the sin of the world upon Him, Christ's pain led Him to question God's heart as well. We must remember that our Heavenly Father turned from Jesus so that He would never have to turn His face away from us. Our pain is paramount to God. The same God who came to rescue His Israelite children from their horrific abusers is the same God who wants to set us free. The faithfulness of God does not mean we will not experience the pain of a broken world and broken people, but that He is always there to hold us, love us, feed us, redeem us, and make us new.

Friend of suffering, I am so sorry for the way your sorrows have snipped away at the threads of your belief in the faithfulness of God. Can I offer to you that whatever deception, depression, or devastation you find yourself in...the arms of I AM, of Jesus, are reaching desperately with compassion, pride, and joy to hold you and call you His own.

Faithful God, I am crying out to You. I am desperate to experience Your arms cradling and supporting me. Open my eyes to behold Your handprints—the ones I never thought were there, the ones the darkness prevented me from seeing. Help me to know and believe that the presence of the enemy doesn't mean the absence of You. I am stepping today on my own "yet this" bridge. My feet are shaky. But I am desperate for my downcast soul to turn upright once again. Help me to sing through my tears, "Great is Your Faithfulness!"

CHAPTER SIX

I Am Power

"And God raised the Lord and will also raise us up by his power."
1 Corinthians 6:14, ESV

"There's only one power in the world great enough to help us rise above the difficult things we face: the power of God."[17]

—Stormie Omartian

We were out of options. There were no more doctor's appointments on the calendar or medications to try. Our Red Sea had been parted the year before when funding and new helpers were provided for Elijah. We were grateful to be "out of Egypt," but we were certainly not in the promised land. This was the wilderness, and I sensed our life would stretch on and on here, just as it did for the Israelites. This was our reality. This was suffering. Not like Anna, not like death, but a complicated, strenuous, and unrelenting kind of sorrow just the same.

It was a typical "breaking furniture" and "breaking spirits" kind of day. The sun was finally down, and so were the kids. Even though my body and mind were exhausted and reached for sleep, my spirit begged for moments awake and alone. I sat in the living room and looked at a framed picture of sleeping baby Lij. Sud-

---

17   Omartian, Stormie. *The Power of a Praying® Woman*. Harvest House Publishers, 2014, p. 14.

denly, I missed him so much I could barely breathe. I ached and longed for him, my son, lost within. I made my way up the stairs as quickly and quietly as I could and opened the door to his room. As I stared at his calm body, breaths coming slow, deep, and rhythmic, I collapsed on the floor next to him. I rocked on my knees with a deep, guttural wail that erupted silently from me like lava. Oh, how I wish I could hold him as a baby once again. He was so easy to comfort and console in a rocking chair with soft, supple skin and milk. A panicked prayer left my lips. It was like all the others in its notes of desperation, but it was the weakest and most deflated in our autism journey thus far: "Jesus, I'm begging you. Heal our little boy. I'll do whatever you ask. Just please help us." A response came quickly, a whisper from His spirit to mine. I grabbed hold of it without hesitation and made the whisper my war cry. Over and over, I chanted, "Release Your Power."

In the days that followed, I couldn't stop thinking we were on the verge of a new and maybe even permanent miracle. But days turned into weeks, and weeks into months, with no power to speak of. As I studied God's power, I halted at Paul's desperate and repetitive prayer in 2 Corinthians 12:8–10 (NIV). I felt like I was staring into a mirror:

> Three times I pleaded with the Lord to take it away from me. But he said to me, "My grace is sufficient for you, for my power is made perfect in weakness." Therefore I will boast all the more gladly about my weaknesses, so that Christ's power may rest on me. That is why, for Christ's sake, I delight in weaknesses, in insults, in hardships, in persecutions, in difficulties. For when I am weak, then I am strong.

Paul begged the Lord to take away his pain, the thorn in his flesh. I begged God to take away Elijah's thorn. It seemed His answer to both of us was the same: "My grace is sufficient for you. My power is made perfect in weakness."

This word for grace (*charis*) means, "that which affords joy, pleasure, delight, sweetness, charm, loveliness; the merciful kindness by which God, exerting his holy influence upon souls, turns them to Christ to keep and strengthen." The word "sufficient" in this text (*arkeō*) means to be possessed of unfailing strength; to be strong, to be enough.[18] With these definitions in mind, "My grace is sufficient" can be otherwise stated, "The merciful kindnesses of God, possessing the soul with unfailing strength… which is enough!"

When the Lord told me to pray "Release Your Power," He was asking me to offer my weakness as an empty plate He could load His sufficient grace upon. I wanted Him to take away the thorn. That was my idea of power. He wanted to give me Himself, the greatest power of all, within the permanence of the thorn.

Sometimes sufficient grace rests on us like a miracle, like the strength to run through the towering walls of the Red Sea. And sometimes, God's sufficient grace looks like manna, also a miracle, but small, predictable, bland, and over time, unexciting. Do we trust and praise Him more when grace is big and shiny versus small and seemingly dull? In our desperation for the outcome we desire, do we accuse God of being deactivated even as He provides the daily manna of His Word and the indwelling Holy Spirit?

Moses's sister Miriam was full of faith and trust as she ran with her people through the miraculously parted Red Sea. In fact, as

---

18 Strong, James. *Strong's Exhaustive Concordance of the Bible.* Thomas Nelson, 1990. Entry G5485, Entry G714.

soon as the water crashed, and the enemy was consumed, she "took a tambourine and led all the women as they played their tambourines and danced. And Miriam sang this song: 'Sing to the Lord, for he has triumphed gloriously; he has hurled both horse and rider into the sea'" (Exodus 15:20–21, NLT). I feel certain she praised God similarly when sufficient grace rained upon the ground, leaving flaky white biscuits. But what about when years went by, and the miracle became unexciting, and when God spoke solely to Moses? Still power, but powerful enough? Here is where both Israel and Miriam crash and burn. Even though God was present in the grace of a cloud by day and fire by night and had face conversations with Moses, Miriam grumbled and complained. She wanted God's power *her* way. She complained about Moses and His prophetic words to her and their people. She complained about God's demonstrations of power. *No God, these graces are NOT sufficient for us. We don't like THIS kind of power.* Miriam was struck with leprosy and sent outside of camp, a week-long reminder that God's provisions were good enough. Even leprosy, a type of thorn in the flesh, was the grace of God, a kind affliction that led toward repentance and dependence. *Miriam, my dear forgetful girl, My grace is unbelievably sufficient for you.*

I've been both Miriams. I've held my tambourine in worship, and I've grumbled with pumping fists to the sky. Manna was a sweet provision and a powerful display of God's love to strengthen His beloved Israel. I can only imagine the wonder-filled day when manna first appeared. Like a first snow, a beautiful, delicious gift of God's abundant grace. Did they marvel at it? Did they dance in it? Day by day, they were physically sustained and strengthened by this gift of grace, but in time, they grumbled at the God who provided it. They also lacked trust in God's promise to provide it continually. They ignored the following instructions:

The Lord said to Moses, "I have heard the grumbling of the Israelites. Tell them, 'At twilight you will eat meat, and in the morning you will be filled with bread. Then you will know that I am the Lord your God.'" That evening quail came and covered the camp, and in the morning there was a layer of dew around the camp. When the dew was gone, thin flakes like frost on the ground appeared on the desert floor. When the Israelites saw it, they said to each other, "What is it?" For they did not know what it was. Moses said to them, "It is the bread the Lord has given you to eat. This is what the Lord has commanded: 'Everyone is to gather as much as they need. Take an omer for each person you have in your tent.' (Exodus 16:11–16, NIV)

God's children traded their faith with fear when they began to gather more than instructed, and maggots rotted the food they collected. Their disobedience and disregard for God's sufficient grace were met with rot. He parted the sea, He spoke in supernatural measures, He answered their hunger with the miraculous, but still, they didn't trust His faithful care for them. They didn't trust that they would wake up to find honey-sweetened manna the next morning.

God gives us His Word, "sweeter than honey to my mouth" (Psalm 119:103, ESV). It is grace. Sometimes we are amazed by it. Sometimes we are grateful for it. Sometimes we complain about it. Sometimes we see it as bland and feel disappointed that it isn't bigger and better. There are also times when we misuse it. I am sadly familiar with this act of misapplying God's Word.

Over and over in the two years before my big breakdown, I

chanted wearily, "I can do all things through Christ who gives me strength" (Philippians 4:13, NIV, paraphrased). I used this verse like a gasoline pump, pulsing it into my heart and body to do all the things I *had* to do instead of stepping back and asking the Lord, "Do you have this for me today?" I assumed all the good and important things were the "all things" I must do, and that God's strength would carry me. I misunderstood His strength. I used His Word to fuel my unhealthy and ungodly expectations for myself: *I can help all the people. I can meet every need of my children. I can say yes to this committee, this ministry, and this person.* I would walk through the kitchen, the store, appointments, and meetings, bleary-eyed and on the edge of tears, chanting, "I can do all things through Christ who gives me strength." But I wasn't listening to God's instructions for me. I was doing more than He was asking me to do. I was gathering more than what was allotted for me. I realize now that doing all those things made me *feel* powerful. People pleasing, performance, and perfection were added daily to my spiritual acts of worship. I wasn't growing stronger, I was getting weaker—all in the name of Jesus. I didn't get it. I wanted the good feeling that came with my accomplishments versus His one grand accomplishment. Eventually, just like the over-collected manna, everything began to rot—including me.

Sometimes the power of God is the strength to wait on Him. Sometimes it's His honey-sweet Word, taken in measure day by day. The Word is Jesus, and His word is our greatest power to possess the soul with unfailing strength. How often do I plead with God to speak to me, to hear His voice, as my Bible sits unopened on the shelf next to me? How often do I beg for something different and new instead of feasting once again on the Bread of Life? Have I forgotten that "the word of God is living and active, sharper than any two-edged sword, piercing to the division of soul and of spirit, of joints and of marrow, and discerning the thoughts and intentions of the heart" (Hebrews 4:12, ESV)? Now *that* is power. Not only do we get to read and ingest it, but by the Spirit it dwells within us. As we depend upon it, we grow stronger. We become filled by the One who is Power.

Paul prayed for the Ephesians to "understand the incredible greatness of God's power for us who believe him. This is the same mighty power that raised Christ from the dead and seated him in the place of honor at God's right hand in the heavenly realms" (Ephesians 1:19–20, NLT). I remember the day in my childhood when I confessed that belief. Yes, He is the Son of God. Yes, I am a sinner, and yes, by His shed blood my sin is pardoned. But this is only the beginning of belief.

When God told Moses that His name was 'I AM,' He was saying 'I AM'—both everything *and* the only thing you need to believe. It is in getting to know the full nature of God that our belief and trust may increase. As the mother of precious Elijah Kelty, I am in charge of scheduling his doctor's appointments and managing his medications. It is my responsibility to organize and participate in his therapy and to champion his education. It is also my job to train our therapy dog, Max. But most importantly, most imperatively to my darling boy, is the regular and consistent prayer for God to release His power. It is this prayer that turns weakness into containers for living water and living bread to fill. It also positions me daily to trust in His power, instead of ordering what kind of power will taste best to me. God is not a vending machine. He is the world's greatest chef, and whatever bread He gives us will always be the best, because it is living. It gives us breath and life like no other substance can.

I learned from my friend Tracey what it truly means to trust

God's power amidst suffering. About three years after losing Anna, I asked her to meet for coffee. I couldn't understand how she exuded peace with God after the tragedy she endured. Her young husband, Dave, and an elderly woman in their church were both diagnosed with the same rare brain tumor simultaneously. A healing service was planned, and both came forward to experience the "releasing of God's power." The older woman was healed, and Dave was not. The unfairness infuriated me. Why didn't God heal them both? Why did Tracey lose her husband and bear the great cost of grief for herself and her young children? I was both confused and pained by the unfair way God both delivered and withheld healing.

How could Tracey sit with me while sharing this story and smile? She was seven years into her loss and radiated so much joy. There was nothing weak about her. So, I asked, "How did you move through the pain and unfairness of God withholding His miraculous power from Dave?" She smiled at me tenderly and gently explained that sometimes God's power comes from His supreme hand, the one that disintegrates tumors and parts seas. Sometimes His power comes from His sufficient hand, the one that settles souls and gives peace. Both hands extend from the God whose power raised Jesus from the dead, and both are good. Each are His attributes, and one cannot be ranked or graded higher than the other.

Tracey went on to tell me about how God's power had filled her home and life in the months and years after Dave died. He didn't take away the grief, but in the vessel of Tracey's weakness, God's sufficient grace was poured out in beautiful, intimate, and satisfying ways. That day was a turning point for me in my grief. God's power, manifested as joy in Tracey, gave me hunger and hope. That day, I began longing for intimacy with God more than with

Anna. It was shocking to me, the desire for God that drummed within me.

Our wilderness with Elijah was teaching me the same thing. But now, it was not only a prayer for me, but for our whole family; a powerful, intimate, satisfying connection with God.

Elijah has the most beautiful eyes, the shape unlike any other Kelty babe. His lashes are dark and long, puckered around each little blue globe, a kiss from the Creator. He is truly beautiful. There are moments when he stares at me, a deep, penetrating look, like he's trying to find me. His overstimulated senses and confused language create a constant fog around him. At times, he places his forehead against mine and looks for the treasure of love in my eyes. Of course, he always finds it. Though a weary flame at times, it burns bright. He can always find me when he tries.

I wish I could always find him. He is a mystery to me so much of the time. What is he thinking? What is he feeling? I nearly go crazy with the ache of longing to know, comfort, and provide for him. But God knows. God holds what I cannot touch, sees what I cannot see, and heals what I will never be able to heal. I can comfort, rock, sing, tickle, play, plan, and pray. That's all I've got, and it's all I've been asked to gather in a day. It's God's measure of a mother's ability, and it weighs an omer. He will do the rest for Elijah and for me. I will seek to rise before the sun and fall asleep with the Word on my tongue. I will continue to pray, "Release Your Power," knowing these words are sent from heaven and they will provide for us. This prayer is a reliable request; it will be answered with sufficient grace—the chef's special manna, in whatever way He chooses to prepare it.

Our wilderness is far from over. As I write today, Elijah is one month from turning thirteen. Our thorn of struggle is still very much with us. Some days it feels normal, and some days it throbs. But it does give us the gift of weakness with which to come to Jesus daily. We get to experience Yahweh as our cloud by day and fire by night. We get to savor His manna, His Word. We look for the ways He is releasing Himself consistently and remember with gratitude the days when new flavors of manna appeared in the wilderness. Like a new laugh that comes from a certain type of joke. Like a new teacher with a special kind of empathy. Like a new connection with a sibling. Like allowing me to pray for him at night again after two years of refusal. In it all, we are continually weak in this desert of ours and consistently filled with the power of God.

I know that as I write about God's power, there must be so many different thoughts and feelings swirling and competing in your heart and mind. Times when you felt God was cruel by withholding power. Or wondered why He didn't intervene as you begged for your prayer to be answered. For your disease to be healed. Your empty womb to be filled. Your marriage to be made whole. For dearest love to arrive. Waiting on the Lord and trusting in His decision-making can feel exhausting and excruciating. But it can also change your life. Our circumstances are not made perfect by His power; rather, His power is made perfect in our weakness. When thorns remain, when prayers go unanswered, when waiting seems to go on forever, we can trust in Jesus, our daily miracle. His supremacy *and* His sufficiency flow with force from the grave He exited. That power is the working of His mighty strength, and it is the same power that dwells in the hearts of those who trust in Him.

God of heaven and God of my heart, You are my miracle. Help me to surrender all my disappointments and sorrows to You and consume me instead with Your sufficient grace. I beg for Your power to be released into my every want, wound, and need. I give to You my deepest longings, my greatest hunger, and my most unbearable despair. I cry out to You, "Jesus, help me! I am weak and needy." Help me to know and believe that God Almighty is my most powerful friend. Help me to continue waiting on You, when my soul demands for better and more. Thank You that daily gratitude for my salvation and the gift of Your Word are the most powerful and sustaining meals I can eat day by day. Give me miraculous inner strength when my thorn throbs and when my heart is tempted to grumble and fight against You. Oh Father, may I know the pleasure and power of Your sufficient grace.

CHAPTER SEVEN

I Am Sovereign

"My purpose will be established, and I will accomplish all My good pleasure."
Isaiah 46:10, NASB

"There is not a square inch in the whole domain of our human existence over which Christ, who is sovereign overall, does not cry: 'Mine!' "[19]
—Abraham Kuyper

The word "control" doesn't flood me with warm, fuzzy feelings. It has always been a scary word for me, attached to those who use control selfishly. Perhaps this is why it was always so hard for me to feel safe in the knowledge of God's sovereign control. To trust and be at peace with God's sovereign authority over all things, we must remind ourselves again and again that I AM is perfect *and* good. In order to rejoice in His "controlling" nature, we have to believe that in all things, God works together for the good of those who love him, who are called according to His purpose (Romans 8:28). It is this God, the one who is both perfect in love and power, that governs our lives. It is easy to esteem God's sovereignty when everything is going well, but what about when everything falls apart?

---

19 Kuyper, Abraham. *Abraham Kuyper: A Centennial Reader*. Edited by James D. Bratt, Wm. B. Eerdmans Publishing Co., 1998, p. 488.

Where I once feared His control, it is now my greatest solace. His authority, paired with His love, means everything will always be alright. In fact, everything will be made beautiful in its time (Ecclesiastes 3:11). The great Author has written many beautiful stories into my life with His sovereign ink. The story that follows is one of my very favorites. It's a love story and like so many, it begins with "Once upon a time, there was a boy…"

I had just turned fifteen, and I sat awkward and afraid, pressed up against the window on the bus headed for Lake Champion. I had signed up to go to Young Life camp alone. The "best week of your life" slogan didn't seem likely at this point. I knew people on the bus, but they weren't my friends. Well, the college leaders were my friends, but that didn't really count. My peers didn't think this preacher's kid was friend material by the time we got to high school. I slumped low and peered up from shielded eyes. *Would I make a friend this week? Who should I befriend and who should I avoid?*

I stared out the window. I watched as the next person to board put a cigarette out on the ground and then climbed the bus steps with an energy that held me. I was instantly drawn to him, not because I thought he could be a friend or shouldn't, just simply because his very presence was magnetic. He hadn't said a word, but I could tell he didn't care what anyone thought of him. He was free in a way I longed to be. Strange and wonderful, all at the same time. He wore dark denim overalls and no t-shirt underneath. I was shocked. Was this a thing? Was this allowed? His style was his own, and the back of the bus cheered when he got on. His hair was as unselfconscious as his personality. It went every which way, the thick, brown, messy strands with bleach-blonde tips. I stared at him like a piece of art I was captured by and couldn't quite understand. I was overcome with curiosity by the charisma that was Jeff Stables.

I watched him all week. He spent most of his time at the smoking pit. Beautiful girls hung on both arms, always. *Who was this guy?* But on the last night of camp, he stood up in a crowd of hundreds and said, "I was out to lunch all my life, but now I'm home. Jesus is my Savior." The entire room erupted in cheers for this guy who had somehow transfixed everyone with his larger-than-life personality and humor. Watching Jeff was like watching a movie I couldn't turn off. I was so happy for this stranger I seemed to care about. So mesmerized by him. He was strange before, but now he was strange and saved, and I was so attracted to him.

It had been a good week, but not the best week of my life. I already believed in God, though believing in a transformative way would come later in my life. I carried sadness all week as I watched groups of kids belonging to each other and felt the emptiness of not belonging to anyone. I stepped onto the bus headed for home and took a seat up front. I hunched low by the window and sank into my sea of loneliness. I was thankful we were riding through the night so I could hide in the darkness. A tear escaped, and I prayed, "Lord, please send someone to sit with me." It was a desperate prayer. For the next ten minutes, happy kids filled every set on the bus but mine.

A moment later, I heard, "Can I sit here?" It was Jeff. For a moment, I just stared. Was he talking to me? Certainly not. But he waited for my reply. I tried not to gape and quickly said yes. Was God answering my prayer for a seat companion with Jeff? He was more awkward one-on-one than I'd imagined. He seemed nervous around me, which was shocking. I learned later that his nerves were because I was a Christian. We were both insecure about the thing the other had that we longed for. He wanted my kind of freedom, and I wanted his. An hour into the trip, he pulled out a sketch book and flipped it open. Now it all made sense. Jeff looked like a piece of art because Jeff was an artist. I marveled at the creation on his lap and the way his pencil worked in his hand. My curiosity trumped my shyness as I blurted, "Who is she?" An intricate pencil drawing of a beautiful girl was on his lap. "The girl I'm in love with," he said. I instantly felt embarrassed, ugly, and… jealous. "She's very pretty," I said. Hours passed, and we both fell asleep. I woke to daylight and Jeff's head on my shoulder. I didn't dare move. A few moments later, he woke up too, and startled, realizing he was using my shoulder as a pillow. We stared at each other for an awkward moment and then quickly turned to face forward. The bus ride home had been the best part of my week, and I wondered if I would ever see Jeff again.

Six weeks later, I stood outside of a similar bus waiting to take a select group of high school kids to another Young Life camp. We would serve on a work crew in various capacities at Windy Gap in Asheville, North Carolina. My older sister had gone on "Work Crew" several years before and made best friends. I was hoping the same would be true for me. As I stood there waiting to see who would be joining from other area high schools, I heard an energetic voice. "It's you," Jeff said, pointing a finger at me from across the parking lot. He hadn't remembered my name, but he did remember *me*.

A couple of days later, about ten of us stood in a circle in the dining hall, gathering to pray for the first set of campers. I was a waitress, and Jeff was a cook. Just before we bowed our heads, someone randomly asked me when my birthday was. "June sixth," I said. Jeff smiled and said, "Me, too." Everyone closed their eyes to pray, but we just looked at each other. Somehow, we knew in that sacred moment that we would become a significant part of each other's lives.

Five years later, after an on-again-off-again romance, in my sophomore year of college at the University of Kentucky, Jeff, in his Junior year at James Madison in Virginia, we broke up. I loved Jeff more than I'd ever loved anyone. Not only did he know and love me, but he helped me to know and love myself. He helped me to see a God he had begun to know in ways that my lies and wounds prevented. But I knew in my heart, though it was killing me, that he wasn't my forever. I wanted it to be Jeff, but he was beginning to feel like a brother. I wept bitterly as I told him we couldn't be "us" anymore. We ended our long-distance phone call, and I fell asleep crying. How could this be right if it felt so wrong?

Eighteen months later, once again swimming in a sea of lone-liness, I was convinced I'd made the biggest mistake of my life. I was coming home from college for the summer and hoped we could rekindle our relationship. Jeff had longed for my freedom from self-hatred. He loved me with God's love, and I soon realized the greatest part of missing Jeff was missing the ways he champi-oned my freedom and led me to Jesus. I didn't realize it at the time, but wanting him was ultimately about needing his truth, needing the ways he'd been the hands and feet of Jesus for so many years.

My hope was destroyed when I learned he had fallen in love with a beautiful artist named Becca, and they were engaged. I cried incessantly. I couldn't imagine how I would live without him. My older brother, Dave, was working for Jeff's painting business that summer. Unbeknownst to me, out of Dave's compassion and love for me, he told Jeff that I was still in love with him. Jeff quickly responded that he would always love me, but that he was *in* love with Becca. Dave shared the news that he hoped would set me free. It felt like death.

Several months later, the Lord brought Chris into my life, and a new love was born. Chris was truly God's intended for me, my truest love. But first love is powerful, and even years into our marriage, I thought of Jeff. It wasn't passion, it was the pain of missing someone that I'd spent years knowing and caring about. Our breakup hadn't changed that. How do you stop caring about someone who changed your life? How do you stop wondering about someone who shaped your soul? How do you stop loving a brother? I felt confused and guilty about my thoughts and found myself surrendering them to Jesus again and again. Only once was there contact through our dear mutual friend, Courtney. When she learned that we had lost Anna, she called Jeff. Later on, Courtney told me, "He cried instantly, Kate. They're praying for you." I was so grateful that he knew and that he still cared enough for me that tears and prayers were offered. I was also deeply touched and somehow relieved to know that his wife would offer prayers for me, too. Grief longs for the tears of friends on its soil, and their tears carried a special kind of comfort deep within.

In March of 2015, I got a call from my sister telling me I needed to sit down. Both of my older siblings were on staff with Young Life. Jeff and his family were also on Young Life staff, stationed in Scotland. "Kristen, what happened? What's wrong?" I couldn't sit. "Katie, Jeff has cancer, and it's not good." I fell on my knees and screamed. She proceeded to share the bad news, and I rocked and wept on the floor. When Chris came home, I shared the awful news, but held it together. Later that night, Chris went to a meeting, and my dear brother knocked on the front door. I opened the door to see Dave's arms outstretched, and I fell into him and sobbed. Jeff was dying, and there was nothing I could do, nothing I could say. I would have to ignore every urge toward compassionate action and grieve alone.

I called my dear Krissy the next day. We cried together on the phone. She understood. She had watched our relationship unfold and had known my ache for him since. Seven months later, I got a call from Courtney: "I received a message that those closest to Jeff should write immediately to encourage him. Kate, you need to write to him." After much prayer and many drafts, I wrote to Jeff, and he wrote back. He said that he *and* Becca were both so grateful for my place in his story of faith.

It was a gift.

It was goodbye.

One month later, Jeff died. He passed away in his childhood home, just miles away from our home in Bridgewater. My mom (who adored Jeff) went to the memorial service with me, and we hid in the back. I watched Becca with her boys. I had longed to see her all these years, and she was even more beautiful than I imagined. I ached for her. I didn't know *this* grief, but I knew grief, and I'd known Jeff, and the combination broke my heart. Her smile amidst sorrow said everything to me about how much she loved both her husband and her God. I wished I could hug her. I wished somehow, I could love her. I timidly signed the guest book and left quickly after the service was over.

One week later, I received a Facebook friend request from Becca. I was shocked. I reached out with love. She reached back with love. *Was this really happening? Were we really doing this?* She was lost, living in an unfamiliar town (my town) without a single friend and clueless about where to enroll her boys for school and where to take them for haircuts. She knew I understood grief and that I'd loved Jeff, and instead of pulling away from me, she drew close. We scheduled coffee. She told me that Jeff once said if we ever met, we would start talking and never be able to stop. He was right. Nine years have passed since that first date, and we're still having coffee. In fact, Becca lives right next door to me on our sleepy cul-de-sac. We are in a group we call "Soul Sisters" with three other women. We share our hearts, our sorrows, our joys, and our lives. Becca is a beloved first-grade teacher and has had three of our children in her class. My husband is more than her neighbor and pastor; he is a dear friend. Becca and Chris talk about books and tidbits I couldn't care less about. She plays and nurtures my children with her adventurous, playful spirit, and I cook meals and tell her handsome sons how much they remind me of their dad. We slip over to each other's houses for coffee before we've even brushed our teeth and walk the neighborhood laughing, crying, and praying. We are now in a season of coming alongside our dearest friends with all comfort as they grieve. It's a marvel. In all my years of wishing I could still be a part of Jeff's life, I never would've imagined that his wife would become a best friend, neighbor, and dear soul sister. But she is, because our Sovereign God is good, and He writes the best stories.

The sweetest thing about the love Jeff and I shared for each other so many years ago was the love of Christ. We were siblings more than anything else. The fact that Becca and I now share that deep sibling love for each other is among the dearest and sweetest gifts of my life. Not only do we understand grief, but we also understand comfort, and we give it generously to one another. The God who is in control of all things steered our lives together and parked us side-by-side–literally. "In *all* things, God works together for the good of those who love him, who have been called according to his purpose" (Romans 8:28, NIV; emphasis added).

The Bible is filled with stories of how God assembled goodness into the broken lives of those He loved and set apart. When Joseph was sold into slavery by his brothers, the Lord was at work. Even as he was hated and cast into a hole by his brothers, God already knew when and how He would lift Joseph up and bring about greatness and glory into his life. Years of slavery and imprisonment were just pieces of a confusing puzzle that would fit together to reveal the spectacular sovereign goodness of God. As years passed, what appeared to be the allowance of evil was, in fact, God setting the stage upon which His kindness and power would be revealed. When Joseph's brothers came begging the Governor of Egypt for food and favor, they had no idea the prominent man before them was the brother they had forsaken. God's grace and greatness is lavished upon them as Joseph concocts a plan for His father to be brought to him as well. When Jacob and his sons were all together again, Joseph bestowed abundance upon them and revealed his identity in saying, "You intended to harm me, but God intended it for good to accomplish what is now being done, the saving of many lives" (Genesis 50:20, NIV).

When Job was afflicted by the enemy's death and destruction, the Lord was at work. He had a plan to restore and bless Job, even as he suffered. But it wasn't immediate, and it wasn't without pain, confusion, and even accusation from Job. He lost everything he loved and worked for. His grief was insurmountable. Can you imagine losing everything, including the people you hold most dear? In Job 42:5–6 (NIV), we hear Job's final declarations about the God who allowed his destruction: "My ears had heard of you but now my eyes have seen you and I repent in dust and ashes." Suffering gave Job the excruciating gift of desperation, which led to dependence, which led to greater knowledge and intimacy with God. The end of Job's life was even more blessed than the beginning. Though death, disease, and evil ransacked his life, God's sovereign plan would not only carry Job through, but restore and redeem his life with goodness. God's sovereign hand is a good hand. Even after all Job had lost, he gained truth, intimacy, and blessing from the Lord.

Both Joseph and Job met the goodness of their sovereign God in suffering. The same God is writing our stories. God takes both the evil and the awful in our lives and weaves His goodness and glory into all of it. Darkness and death are invitations for the good author to bring light and life, and that is exactly what He does.

Jeff left a cavernous hole filled with sorrow. It is also filled with the presence, power, and goodness of God, who resurrected my dear brother to eternity. This is the sovereign goodness of God.

God's sovereignty is a comfort when we understand He is in loving control, but His control can also feel terrifying. We don't want him to drive us through sickness, suffering, or grief. How can we make peace and receive comfort from the God who allows the hard and even the heinous things?

Do you ever struggle to feel like God's sovereignty and His goodness contradict each other? In your suffering, have you asked, "How can the God of perfect love allow such imperfect things?"

Just a few months after Anna died, I timidly and tearfully sat in the kitchen with my daddy. His empathy for me and his understanding of theology led me to confess, "God's sovereignty feels terrifying to me. What does it all mean?" He tenderly explained to His grieving girl that God's sovereignty means that nothing takes Him by surprise, that all things are under His loving control. His omniscience (all-knowing God), His omnipresence (all-present God), and His omnipotence (all-powerful God) are the components of His sovereignty. He explained that God's sovereignty and

His goodness cannot be separated from one another and that we see His ultimate sovereignty displayed at the cross.

I wonder, was there ever a moment when Jesus, consumed with excruciating physical and spiritual pain on the cross, questioned the sovereignty of His Father and His God?

"My Father, if it is possible, let this cup of suffering be taken from me..." (Matthew 26:39, NLT). *Can You please author the good news in a way that doesn't inflict pain and devastation upon Me?* These words were first spoken by King David in the first verse of Psalm 22. On the cross, Jesus quotes David and also fulfills a prophecy (Matthew 27:46). His cry isn't a question so much as it is an answer to the moan of every mourning soul for all time: *Why God, Why?*

Our stories are lived under the canopy of the greater story, which is the life, death, and resurrection of dearest Jesus. The sovereign goodness of God wrote the painful yet perfect story of what we now call the gospel. The trip from heaven to earth and back again had to be driven straight through Calvary and hell so that Jesus might be able to take us home with Him. He wrote and lived the hardest story so that all our stories could be lived to the fullest. He said, "...I have come that they may have life, and have it to the full" (John 10:10, NIV). That abundance was manifested by His submission and obedience unto death. "...not my will, but yours be done" (Luke 22:42, NIV)

This is how Jesus followed His plea for a way other than suffering. "For the joy set before him he endured the cross..." (Hebrews 12:2, NIV). This is what Jesus held in His heart and mind and why He accepted God's sovereign ink, His very own blood. He surrendered sovereignty because of the ultimate goodness of you and me restored to Him; the joy of you and me, embodied by His spirit; the joy of you and me, comforted in death; the joy of you and me, forever with Him. He lived the hardest story so we could live the greatest. This is why God's sovereignty matters. This is why His control is also His love and His goodness. They cannot be separated from one another; rather, they flow in and out of each other. He wrote pain to the uttermost into His own story so we could be saved to the uttermost, and it was all scripted from the quill of His son's willing blood flowing with greatest love. They cannot be separated from one another; rather, they flow in and out of each other.

Last spring, Becca and I went to a greenhouse together to buy plants and flowers for our yards. We walked together, and each of us picked out the petals and colors that spoke to us. We spent the afternoon pulling weeds, digging into the dirt, and planting beauty for ashes. I was overcome by our side-by-side life. It hit me all over again—the enormous gift in what has become so normal. With dirt under our nails and new flowers to show, we beheld what the other had done by sunset.

Thirty years ago, I sat sad and lonely on a camp bus and prayed for a friend. On that day, God gave me Jeff, *and* He also gave me Becca. In the same moment he planted Jeff in my life, He also saw the day Becca and I would be planting flowers in the soil we share. God sees the tears we will shed together in the future and the ways we will champion one another's families in support and prayer. He sees our children growing and our hair graying and the seasons ahead when we will "sister" each other in the hard and holy. He sees the day when heaven will give us our loves once again, and as Becca says, we will delight in the beauty and joy of seeing one another "soul to soul." The sovereignty of I AM is the goodness of I AM, and in it all… we are held in His unfailing love.

Friend: Has the sovereignty of God confused, evaded, or infuriated you? You are not alone! In the years when I couldn't see or feel God's kindness in death and grief, the only comfort I had was in reflecting on those who suffered before me and not only survived, but thrived. One of the nurses who took care of me when Anna died shared that her first baby was born still, eighteen years earlier. She sat on the bed with me as I wept uncontrollably. In her eyes, I saw pain, but in her hand, I felt support. In her life, I found hope. In time, she had other children. She changed career paths and became a nurse so she could support other grieving parents. She also shared with me that when she moved into her new home, her baby's ashes sat securely in her lap in the car, not in the moving truck. Time and years had given her courage, purpose, and fulfillment. I was comforted that the presence of God's goodness didn't eradicate her love for her first baby. The thought of her "moving on, but with" was a thought that gave me hope. I, too, would learn how to move on in life, but with love for Anna secure in my lap.

I cannot begin to tell you how many times I clutched the memory of her when consumed with despair. I would tell myself, "One day I will be like her." God's sovereign hand, the one that allowed my pain, also extended to me every beautiful, wonderful gift in my life today. Anna's ashes sit on my dresser in a small velvet-lined wooden box. My love for her has grown right alongside the goodness of God. Yes, what the enemy meant for evil can and will be turned for our good. Do you know a suffering survivor, someone you can look up to, where God's goodness amidst pain has been displayed? Both God's Word and this world are filled to the brim and overflowing with those who have been marked with both grief *and* goodness. One day, you will be a soul like that, too. Can I invite you to come to the throne of grace with confidence in your time of need, to be honest before Sovereign I AM, and let

Him rescue you with His promises? He is making a way for you, even now as you read these words. His sovereign pen is writing goodness and mercy all the days of your life, and this too shall pass into a season of greater redemption and joy.

Jesus, You endured the cross for me. You suffered so that my suffering could be held and restored by Your love, goodness, and victory. Jesus, I need the gospel I've known for so long to grow deeper, stronger roots, causing me to grow and heal in ways I desperately need and can barely imagine. Thank You that You didn't run away in fear from the sovereign plan that saved my life and gave me the gift of Your presence, power, and love. Protect me from my fears, doubts, and accusations. Give me the gift of knowing the secrets of Your heart—the ones that will lead me to say, "for the joy set before me and for the goodness I believe is God, I can and will endure this, my daily cross." Help me to trust Your ink and authorship over my story even when darkness, sorrow, pain, betrayal, and grave disappointment mar the page. Thank You for being my perfect ending and ever-present hope. Oh, how I love and need You, Sovereign I AM.

CHAPTER EIGHT

I Am Truth

"...If you abide in my word, you are truly my disciples, and you will know the truth, and the truth will set you free."

John 8:31–32, ESV

"My feelings are not God. God is God. My feelings do not define truth. God's word defines truth. My feelings are echoes and responses to what my mind perceives. And sometimes—many times—my feelings are out of sync with the truth. When that happens—and it happens every day in some measure—I try not to bend the truth to justify my imperfect feelings, but rather, I plead with God: Purify my perceptions of your truth and transform my feelings so that they are in sync with the truth."[20]

—John Piper

There was a chill in the air, and the crunch of autumn under my little five-year-old feet. The wooded path carried me and Mama to this promised date I'd begged and longed for. It was our time, our breakfast picnic in the woods that graced the edge of our cul-de-sac, this forest which offered daily adventure and a match to my imagination. Our picnic had been long anticipated. The youngest of three children, I was always eager for any one-on-one time with my mom.

---

20 Piper, John. *You Are God's Midwife for the New Birth of Others.* Desiring God, 29 Apr. 2007, www.desiringgod.org/messages/you-are-gods-midwife-for-the-new-birth-of-others.

My hair was neatly braided into two pigtails. If I closed my eyes tight and imagined my blondish-brown hair was red, I was at once Anne Shirley, my literary hero. She was much more than a girl in a book to me. She was all spunk and spirit and made me feel like Green Gables existed for me, too. I wasn't the only one who got in trouble and who exasperated those around her with her wild imaginings, unequaled curiosity, and self-will. If only the leaves falling to the ground were from sprawling trees in the forest of Avonlea and not a cul-de-sac off Boulder Brook Drive in the suburbs of Atlanta, Georgia. When I convinced myself I was just like Anne, I didn't feel all alone in being "bad." There was even a hint that her type of "bad" could be beautiful. As we walked to the woods together, I saw Mama watching me with wonder. Her delight in my uncontained and unmeasured "Katie-ness" tempted me to think… *perhaps I am good?* But that thought didn't last because *he* came. He always came. My kidnapper.

It was as if he stood in the shadows, waiting for those moments when he saw that I was happy and unhindered. He never allowed me to forget "who I really was." He was good at being cruel, always branding and rebranding his scarlet letter upon my tiny soul. I didn't know at the age of five who this kidnapper was, just that in his presence, I wanted to run away from myself. Whenever he came, I was consumed with what I now know to be shame, guilt, and fear. I couldn't name those emotions as a child. I only knew they were bad. So, whenever they grabbed me, I thought of them as the "B" feelings (B for bad).

As an adult, I have been able to unmask this kidnapper and see him for who he really is. Jesus describes him as "…a murderer from the beginning, not holding to the truth…When he lies, he speaks his native language, for he is a liar and the father of lies" (John 8:44, NIV). The kidnapper first appears in Genesis. His target is God's children. He lied to Adam and Eve about their Father to lure them away from trust and truth. He deceived them, inserting doubt, fear, and desire. They took the enemy's hand when they took that apple, the devil's candy. All at once, Adam and Eve were consumed by their own "B" feelings. They were harassed with shame, and they hid from God.

Have you ever hidden because of shame? What are the "B" feelings that make you want to run away and hide from others, from God, from yourself?

My "B" feelings originate with early memories of sexual abuse and emotional trauma. I know now that when children experience trauma, they often make another's sin *their* sin to try to fix what they can't control. I didn't have the ability to see adults as anything other than "good." Therefore, this bad thing that happened to me must be because "I was bad."

As I grew up, the "B feelings" became "B phrases." *I am gross. I am hideous. Something is wrong with me.* I feared that just as I'd been hurt, I could hurt others. I feared that perhaps I was dangerous. The pain and fear of these phrases were torturous. But sweet Mama was always ready to tell me the truth:

"A is for Adorable. Katie is adorable."

"B is for Brave. Katie is brave."

"C is for creative. Katie is creative." On and on she went from A to Z, lifting my heart from the ground, giving a new and real definition to who I was. I didn't realize it at the time, but Mom was using the only weapon against the Father of Lies. She wielded her sword and demolished every lie that set itself up against the knowledge of God (2 Corinthians 10:5). I got used to going to Mama so she could stab the lies for me. Mama kept me safe.

I wish I could tell you that shame disappeared after that. Unfortunately, the voice of the accuser has followed me all my life. At fifteen, another kidnapper came. He was five years older than I. A man who took me under his dark wings and turned me into an object. He was sexually and emotionally abusive. He ranted about my body and what it should look like and how he expected me to become his version of perfect. By the time I turned seventeen, I was forty-five pounds thinner, and my heart was emaciated, too. I barely ate, I exercised obsessively, and took as many as fifteen laxatives a day to make sure nothing was ever in my system. I would stare naked in the mirror and chant, "You are ugly, you are hideous, you are bad." These verbal lashes forced me to submit to shame and motivated me toward the physical punishments of anorexia.

I wasn't as keen on Mama's voice then. In fact, just like Eve, I hid in my shame and self-hatred. In college, I renewed my faith and began crying out to Jesus, but my controlling behaviors turned to spiritual legalism. I would prove that I was good to others and to myself. I would make up for all my badness. I would make amends. More years went by—greater pursuit of Jesus. Greater healing. But the dirty lie about how dirty I really was kept hissing from the shadows: When Anna died, *it's your fault, you are bad.* When Elijah was diagnosed with autism, *it's your fault; your womb is broken.* When our marriage suffers under stress, *you are the problem. You are bad.* When I look in the mirror and don't see the shape of the girl I once was, *you hold shame under your skin. You are bad.*

How do we break the power of these lies? How do we live into the truth of who we are in Christ? If Mama's voice could lessen the pain of my shame and fear, what could the most powerful voice in the world accomplish?

Jesus said this to His disciples: "So Jesus said to the Jews who had believed him, 'If you abide in my word, you are truly my disciples, and you will know the truth, and the truth will set you free'" (John 8:31–32, ESV).

A few years ago, I began intensive trauma therapy, seeking to unhear and stop listening to the voice that defined me as bad. Session after session, my therapist, Dana, would tell me the truth: "You are not bad. Bad things happened to you. Those bad things are not your fault. You are loved. You are good." One day, as I meditated on Dana's words to me, I began to feel smothered and trapped in darkness. I asked the Lord to rescue me from this moment of despair. An image came to mind, a light growing bigger and bigger until I saw myself seated in front of a campfire, leaning back against Jesus. I felt safe and warm. Then Jesus began drawing in the sand. He wrote my name, "Katherine." But then, under that, He wrote another name. He wrote "Agatha." It startled me. Who was Agatha? I didn't find it to be a pretty name. In fact, I decided it was a bad name. The panic returned as I thought disappointedly on the fact that God thought of me as an "Agatha."

In my next counseling session, I shared this experience with Dana. She asked if I had looked up the meaning of the name Agatha. I hadn't. Dana got out her phone and searched. She began reading and then gasped, immediately pressing her hand to her heart. With tears in her eyes, she said to me, "Kate. Agatha means *good*."

She said it slowly and deliberately. She stared deep into my eyes and into my history. She stared, searching until she found me, little Katie, the one who had followed the voice of another shepherd into the deepest, deceiving woods of shame. She kept nodding her head, hand on heart, waiting for me to join her in the miracle that we were standing in. I stared at her blankly for three more seconds, and then, I heaved. I clutched my chest in disbelief and gratitude. It was as if the Good Shepherd had come to rescue His little lost lamb from the one who had kidnapped me. My Good Shepherd, who calls me His beloved sheep, His redeemed daughter, His good girl.

There is another woman who experienced Jesus writing in the sand as the enemy chanted her badness. When the Pharisees presented this sexually shameful woman to Jesus to see if He would uphold the stoning law, His reply was simple. He bent down and wrote on the ground. When they questioned Him again, Jesus replied, "Let him who is without sin among you be the first to throw a stone at her." After this proclamation, He returns to the very peculiar task of writing in the dirt. One by one the crowd walks away. Jesus rises from the ground to face the woman and says, "'Woman, where are they? Has no one condemned you?' She said, 'No one, Lord.' And Jesus said, 'Neither do I condemn you; go, and from now on sin no more'" (John 8:3–11, ESV).

The first time we see God with His hands in the dirt is to create man. The second time we see God bend to gather earth, He makes mud to heal the blind man. Before His death, we see Jesus bend to engage with dirt by washing it off His disciples' feet. Jesus has a special relationship with dirt. By it, He creates, heals, and cleans. We don't know what Jesus wrote in the sand as He bent at the adulterous woman's feet, but we can know that the One who bends to the dirt does so with a posture to create and to clean.

Jesus rises from the ground to face the woman, *and* He rises from the ground to face you and me. Our God, who made dirt, who created children from dirt, who heals and cleans with dirt and remembers we are from dirt, and who descended into dirt and rose from the dirt, gets to have the first and final word. It is His very first appraisal of man in the garden: "Very good!" (Genesis 1:31, NIV). And for the dependent sheep, it will be His last word as well: "Well done, *good* and faithful servant" (Matthew 25:23, NIV; emphasis added)—enter the joy of the Lord. The word "good" in this text is the Greek word *agathós*.[21] Sound familiar? This is where the name *Agatha* is derived. When Jesus allowed my spirit to watch as He wrote my name anew in the sand, it was the same silent, sin-scathing speech He gave to the adulterous woman: "You are *now* good." We crave this affirmation because it's the first word He ever spoke over us. He set our identity in motion with this word centuries ago.

Horrifically, the enemy has defiled our name. He shot his arrow of sin and death straight through the message of our perfect value in Eden, and we are each born with a terminal problem. We are "sinful from birth" (Psalm 51:5, NIV). The miracle of salvation is that when we see ourselves clearly as diseased and drowning masterpieces, we have access to His saving and cleansing blood. When we repent and surrender our lives to God, a holy transfusion takes place. A miraculous cleansing as His pure blood surges into ours. This is the moment of complete and permanent purification. We are born once again, and our "very good" nature is restored. This doesn't turn us into an army of glory robots. We are each a unique masterpiece, with unique DNA. Our surrender to the Creator and His blood ignites the true life we were born to live: an abundant life for His glory.

---

21 Strong, James. *Strong's Exhaustive Concordance of the Bible*. Thomas Nelson, 1990. Entry G18.

Unfortunately, the enemy doesn't give up when salvation re-names us. He seeks to lure newborn and growing children of God into the thrashing waters of sin. We will certainly have moments when we give in to temptation and tune our ear to the deceiver, but this doesn't change us from good back to bad. We just become dirty. How quickly can we submerge ourselves in His cleansing and replenishing living water? How quickly can we declare, "The eternal God is your refuge, and underneath are the everlasting arms. He will drive out your enemies before you, saying, 'Destroy them!'" (Deuteronomy 33:27, NIV). Every advance of the enemy can be boiled down to shame. There isn't a soul on this earth who the enemy doesn't target with *this* B feeling. For each of these souls, God is desperate to drive out the enemy and to declare "Destroy." I have never sat with someone who didn't have a shame story to tell me. What is yours? In what ways has the kidnapper sought to lure your heart away from the Good Father who longs to redeem, rewrite, and remind you of your true and lasting identity written in the sand?

Jesus says, "So Jesus said to the Jews who had believed him, 'If you abide in my word, you are truly my disciples, and you will know the truth, and the truth will set you free" (John 8:31–32, ESV). To abide means to rest within—to make oneself at home—to recline into the security and love of Jesus, enjoying the fire He's built just for you. The one called I AM enlightens, warms, and refines. As I write, I recall the beloved disciple John and how he leaned back against Jesus' chest at the last supper. The King James Version says, "Now there was leaning on Jesus' bosom one of his disciples, whom Jesus loved" (John 13:23). Can you imagine feeling so safe, loved, and desiring of Jesus that you would lean back resting your full weight upon Him, your head on His chest? As we imagine and visualize what is true, new neural pathways are created in our brains, opening new highways of truth that lead to freedom.

Can I invite you to lean back against Jesus now as the beloved disciple did? Listen to His heartbeat. Listen to His voice: *I made you. I delight in you. I died for you. I am living for you. I am longing for you. I am waiting for you. I am victory and freedom for you. I am the Way, the Truth, and the Life for you. Run to me and come home to the Father. Come home to I AM and leave all your shame behind.*

Dearest Father, ever-present Truth, I beg of You, set me free. Teach me what it means to abide in You and to love doing so. Teach me what it means to cling to the voice of my Good Shepherd and to run from the voice of any other. Heal the parts of me where shame has festered infection. Heal the parts of me that are sick from deception. Thank You that you write in the sand a new name and a new identity just for me. Thank You for remembering that I am made of dust. You are a gentle and patient Creator that recreates newness within me each time I come to You. Thank You that I can look up to You with gratitude and love and say, "No one has condemned me." Help me to leave behind the life of sin and my partnership with the accusatory voice that seeks to hurt, not help me. I choose You, Jesus, just as You have chosen me. I need You; I love You, precious I AM.

CHAPTER NINE

I Am Peace

"Peace I leave with you; my peace I give to you. I do not give to you as the world gives. Do not let your hearts be troubled and do not be afraid."

John 14:27, NIV

"God cannot give us a happiness and peace apart from Himself, because it is not there. There is no such thing.[22]

—C.S. Lewis

"Katie, I need you," she wept into the phone.

It was early in the morning, and I was still dripping wet from my shower.

"Krissy? What's wrong? Where are you?" My heart was throbbing.

"I'll tell you when you get here. I'm at Massanetta on the hill," she cried. "Please come quickly."

I threw on my clothes as fast as I could and raced out the door with sopping wet hair. I needed to get to my Krissy. It was May of 1999. I had just come home from my second year of college at the University of Kentucky, and I was desperate to be with my kindred spirit. We hadn't been together since Christmas. Her

---

22 Lewis, C. S. *Mere Christianity*. HarperOne, 2001, p. 50.

phone call early that morning pushed our scheduled date up several hours. I got to Massanetta Springs quicker than I ever had before. This was our sacred "growing up" spot. From camp days to church picnics, to teenage nights spent swapping secrets on the dock. We would come here both together and alone. It was our place to hold hands with each other and with God.

As kids, we enjoyed canoeing on the lake, but as we got older, we preferred the dock, staring, like guests at a museum, taking in our favorite piece of art. The most enormous weeping willow graced the bank. It told us it was safe to cry here, to seek shelter here. From this spot, we looked up the hill beyond the water. It rolled perfectly, reminding us we were Virginia valley girls. Though we never said it, we both knew we were lifting our eyes to the hill, the place where our greatest help came from (Psalm 121:1–2).

I parked at the dock and saw her at once, so small and folded up. I started running, and she stood, arms outstretched. I swept her tiny little frame into my body and enveloped her. I could breathe again now that we were together. Krissy's heart was breaking. Love was involved and a decision. She was anxious and afraid. I don't remember much about the words we shared, just that over the next hour, we were guests of honor on this holy hill. We wept together, we prayed, and we held hands until there was nothing left to say. The sky above us was the perfect shade of blues, and the pure puffs of cotton clouds were abundant. The spring breeze wrapped around us, the coolness and yet hopefulness of the season inviting us both to something new. The earlier feelings of panic had left Krissy as she let herself rest in God's presence and His promises to guide and sustain her. The lake below was home to one single elegant swan who was always there and always perfect. Our feathered friend floated, being moved entirely by the current underneath her. We were floating now too, still and yet moving in a rhythm of grace. I wish the moment could've been painted. It would be called Peace.

This was not the last time Krissy called me in a panic. Eighteen years later, with full lives and big families, I answered her call. Her voice was just as soft and sweet as ever, and yet there was something awful hiding in her hello. Something that shot terror through every part of me.

"Krissy, what's wrong?"

She said it quickly. "I'm having brain surgery."

This was not a sentence I could process. This was not a sentence that was allowed to be real. I stopped breathing.

"They found a tumor."

Breathe Kate.

"They hope it's benign."

Breathe Kate! Breathe!

"Do you remember a few months ago when we had lunch and I asked so many questions about Becca and Jeff? So much curiosity about how she and her children were doing since his death. So many questions about heaven?"

Please Kate… breathe, breathe, breathe.

"Katie, is God preparing me for my death?"

At that remark, fiercest love surged in my blood, and sudden breath inflated my lungs.

"Kristin Noelle, you listen to me! That is fear talking and nothing more." I was adamant. I was commanding. I was afraid.

We spent the next thirty minutes processing, emoting, and praying. I repeatedly told her everything was going to be okay because that's what best friends do and because it *had* to be okay. It was my turn to be faithful, to be "emunah" for Kristin. It was my turn to hold her arms steady. Kristin was the loving wife and mother of four children. She was the most present, nurturing woman I'd ever known. She read the classics to her babies and gently traced their backs as they lay in her lap. I would often watch her and take mental notes. She embodied beauty and grace. There was no way a woman as lovely as this could be sick, but she was.

Over the next few months, I traveled the one-hour trip many times over the mountain to Charlottesville. Sometimes Krissy felt well, and we would sit, talk, and daydream about house renovations. Some days, treatment made her feel so awful, she slept while I cleaned the house and rocked the baby. There were some days when the tears flowed so freely for us both I was certain we would drown. The drive home over the mountain was always scary. I would let out all the emotions I didn't want Krissy to see. The fear, anger, and grief that came in wails and screams along the highway.

On one such evening, I drove home and immediately collapsed on my bed in panicked grief. I felt crushed and squeezed. I couldn't calm down under the pain of losing her, under the pain of watching her suffer, under the pain of watching her husband, friends, family, and children hurt. Leaving her felt wrong. I had the notion to set up a tent in her front yard and abandon everything else in my life. But that was impossible. I wish we could've just lived on "our hill." That felt safe, manageable, and treatable compared to this.

I closed my eyes and begged God for help. At once, an image came to me. Krissy and I were together, holding hands like usual, but instead of being in her home or on the hill, we were petrified at the bottom of the ocean. We looked at each other, desperate and terrified, knowing our breath was about to run out. But then Jesus appeared under the water with us. "Breathe," He said. As we joined our hands with His, suddenly, we *could* breathe. The panic vanished as peace swelled in us, around us, and upon us. Peace transcended our ability and our understanding.

It felt as though cancer was a cruel hand holding us both under the water as we kicked and flailed. "Jesus, we are drowning," I thought. But then, my imagination was joined with God's Spirit, and I faintly saw Jesus under the water, inviting us to breathe into what was humanly impossible. The Scripture came to mind, "We are afflicted in every way, but not crushed; perplexed, but not driven to despair; persecuted, but not forsaken; struck down, but not destroyed; always carrying in the body the death of Jesus, so that the life of Jesus may also be manifested in our bodies" (2 Corinthians 4:8–10, ESV). The image, along with the verse, encompassed me like a life vest and sent me gasping to the surface.

I pondered the truth received under the water; *the life and breath of Jesus were with us, even as cancer pressed us down.* Suddenly, I knew I could do this. I could suffer with and for Kristin while manifesting the resurrected Jesus in my spirit and body.

The next week, when I visited Kristin, I shared this holy moment with her. I told her that every time I prayed for her now, I imagined holding her hand under the deep waters of this awful cancer. I told her I took deep breaths for us both and imagined her sickness and weakness overcome by the power and peace of God. I could barely get the words out as I sought to speak through such heavy emotion. She looked at me, almost stunned, and said, "Katie, I knew you loved me deeply, but I don't think until this moment I realized how deep." It was a precious moment, sacred, and I knew I would cherish it forever.

My dear Krissy spent the last week of her life in a beautiful hospice house. I followed the ambulance in my car that took her from the hospital to her "final home." I walked into her room shortly after she arrived and watched as several nurses helped her to the bed. Upon seeing me, she smiled brightly and weakly whispered to the staff, "My sister is here; this is my sister."

"It's so nice to meet Kristin's sister," the nurse responded. I corrected her, and in a way, apologized for the error. "Actually, we are dear, lifelong friends." Kristin's sweet smile disappeared, and she softly and sorrowfully chided me, "We *are* sisters." My heart sank. "Yes, Krissy, we are sisters." Oh, how I wish I could redo that moment.

My final goodbye with my sister was among the most sacred moments of my life. I climbed into her bed and curled my body around her small, fragile frame. She was no longer able to walk, eat, or talk. She just was. There were moments of "coming to" and soft, short words spoken, but life as my dear one had known it was gone. Courtney and Laurie, best friends from college, were there, too. Courtney sat at her feet, and Laurie sat at her side. We encircled our beloved friend and filled the room with immeasurable love and pain. We weren't sure how aware she was or what she could hear, but I became overcome with the sense that I should speak to her.

I whispered in her right ear everything I could think to say. I told her all about her loves, her sweet babies, and her husband and how they were doing—how God was already meeting their deep needs. I told her about the funeral arrangements being made and the beautiful flowers that were being ordered, her very favorites, peonies and hydrangeas, in blush pinks and shades of white. I told her how much God loved her and how proud and loved He felt by all the ways she trusted and depended on Him in sickness and death. I told her that very soon she would begin to see His face, His immense delight, and pleasure in her. That she would experience the unconditional love we longed to know and feel fully all our lives. I told her heaven was waiting and that it would take her breath away. I told her Anna was waiting and her grandparents.

When I was all out of words, we sang hymns to our Krissy. And then, we were quiet. At once, Courtney noticed Kristin's brow furrow. We winced at the pain she felt. But then she slowly reached up and touched her earlobe and whispered a single word. Courtney understood her immediately and said, "Kate, she said 'voice.' She wants to hear your voice. Keep talking to her." I nestled even closer to her and began to speak again. She breathed deeply, her brow lines disappeared, and she was serene once more. I spoke until Krissy was asleep. I looked down at the place where our hands were gently clasped. I knew it was the last time I would ever hold her hand. I kissed her cheeks profusely and lay as close, but as gently, to her as I could. Krissy was now like our swan; perfectly still and yet moving heavenward upon the current of His love. As painstaking as it was, it was the second time in my life when I wished a moment could be painted. This, too, would be called "Peace."

"Finally, brothers and sisters, whatever is true, whatever is noble, whatever is right, whatever is pure, whatever is lovely, whatever is admirable—if anything is excellent or praiseworthy—think about such things. Whatever you have learned or received or heard from me, or seen in me—put it into practice. And the God of peace will be with you" (Philippians 4:8–9, NIV).

The word peace, "eirēnē," is derived from the word "eiro'," a verb which means "to join."[23] Peace is multi-faceted. In its outer

---

23 Strong, James. *Strong's Exhaustive Concordance of the Bible*. Thomas Nelson, 1990. Entry G1515.

layer, we feel and experience it. That, of course, is when we like it the most. But before peace is a feeling, it's a partnership. At the very core of peace, there is a joining with I AM. When we lace our lives together with His, we are given the deepest and most foundational layer of peace—eternal confidence and Spirit-filled living. In this way, we can also experience peace as a fruit and as a gift of abiding in Him. That's when peace can transcend all understanding and guard our hearts (Philippians 4:7), and rule in our souls (Colossians 3:15).

I didn't realize it at the time, but my last whispers in Kristen's ear were a list of true, noble, pure, lovely, admirable, excellent, and praiseworthy things. I was reminding Krissy who she was joined to, and meditating on those things gave her peace. Krissy died amongst the horrors of death with a smile on her face. This is the fulfillment of greatest peace. This is the deepest and truest partnership made visible.

Jesus suffered from anxiety that dripped as blood-filled sweat. In the Garden of Gethsemane, He begged God to spare Him the crucifixion. Jesus, fully God, felt the agony of fear and worry in His human body. But ultimately, He yielded to death and resurrected from it. In doing so, He was then able to extend His life-saving hand to us. When we reach back for the hand that is reaching for us, we are joined to Peace. Jesus, the Prince of Peace, takes up residence in our bodies, minds, and souls. We are joined to, embedded with, and empowered by a peace hero, a ruling war champion. When my husband leaves for a trip and I don't feel him, it doesn't change the fact that I am his wife and take great comfort and security in the ways we are joined, even when we are apart. This is how it is with peace. It is the Christian's identity. It is who we are because of Who we are joined to, and at times we enjoy the feel of it, but not always. There are times as a believer when we feel anything but peace, but that doesn't change the reality that we are ultimately at peace and in peace because of our partnership with Abba.

Have you known a season where your strongest partnership was with pain? Krissy felt that until the day she died. She also felt cradled again and again by Peace. I think being a child of God in "opposite of peace" seasons and circumstances, is resting in Jesus' words: "In this world you will have trouble. But take heart (have courage)! I have overcome the world" (John 16:33, NIV).In other words, *I am your champion, and I will carry your heart and soul into the place where peace is the very air you breathe, but until then, I am breathing in you.* When we meditate on the truth that the breath of God is our present and future reality, we are inviting peace to permeate every horrific feeling and force within this life. It's glorious when we get to *feel* it, but *knowing* we are soul-joined with the One named Peace, we will find an anchor in the fiercest storm.

Several months after losing Kristin, I made my way to Massanetta. I wept the whole way there, knowing what was before me. I walked all our childhood paths, making sure to stop at the Spring House. I walked along the stream, remembering how we skipped in our dresses barefoot after Sunday picnics. I remembered all the ways we were a song, how our melodies and harmonies mingled. I remembered how our sass, spunk, and imaginations were the perfect puzzle of "us." I remembered all our dock moments. Now, here I was again, so many years had passed, and without her.

As I walked up the hill, walking up to a memory, I felt the pain of never sweeping her little frame into my arms again. I was undone, lying now in the grass, curled up, weeping and missing my kindred spirit. What was I to do without her friendship, her acceptance, reassurance, faithfulness, and love? What was I to do without her voice and her hand? I wept until every tear for that moment was shed. I talked to the sky, I talked to Jesus. I left exhausted by sorrow but filled with… peace. I had spent my afternoon grieving and mourning, but joined with God. Yes, peace is a partnership.

In the months that followed, I was hit by a new type of worry. Had I loved her well enough? Had I failed her in any way? It was an unrelenting and searing type of panic. As I prayed for relief from that awful fear, I had my first dream of Kristin.

We were standing together in the hallway of the church where we grew up. I was on the floor panicking and cutting out hearts from red and pink construction paper. "What are you doing?" she asked me. I didn't turn to look at her, but just kept right on cutting out hearts at rapid speed. "I must keep cutting. I can't stop," I said. Then she called my name: "Katie." That stopped me. I could *hear* her smile. The tenderness in her voice was an invitation. I turned to her and gasped. She stood above me, so beautiful, so new, so well— and alive. With her thick brown hair flowing, she wore a beautiful white dress that fit her like a glove. I knew it had been made just for her. Her right hand was over her heart. "Look," she said. At that, she removed her hand and revealed that underneath was one of my hearts, the reddest one. She was wearing it like a treasured badge. "You can stop now," she said. "This will always be here."

I woke up in both the pain of having seen her so clearly and missing her so terribly, but with new peace. The dream Jesus gave me allowed me "to join" to the most lovely, pure, and right reality. I had loved my sister to the best of my ability, and our love was permanent. It would be redeemed in eternity. Though death had taken her from me physically, we could never be spiritually disconnected because we were joined by Him.

God's love and providence carried Kristin and me through more than thirty years together. From the time we were a shepherd and Mary in our 1986 Christmas pageant to the church choir and high school musicals. From curling up together in a cold church in inner city Philly on a mission trip, to beach vacations and so many letters back and forth through college. Through the death of my child and the agony of her infertility, and through cancer. Want to know the truth? I still hold her hand. I love how the Bible tells us that we are seated today in heavenly places (Ephesians 2:6). Sometimes, when I am completely overwhelmed and struggling to find peace, I close my eyes and imagine holding her hand. We are not on our hill, or under water, or in that holy hospice bed. We are side by side in the kingdom of heaven. We are joined by Jesus, and from this very real, but unseen posture, I pray like we always did. I pray for her children and for my own. In this way, I connect myself to all that is so very true, noble, pure, lovely, admirable, excellent, and praiseworthy. This is how I welcome the feeling of peace from my partnership with peace. This is how I love my Krissy and rest in the pain of her absence. This is how I align with my true citizenship in heaven and escape the pain of being temporarily joined to this world.

I can only imagine all the ways you are fractured and crumbling, friend of suffering. I am immensely sorry for the ways your unrelenting circumstances make peace seem elusive. I am so sorry for the ways your unanswered prayers grab hold of doubt and fear. I am so sorry for the way your body diseases and mind diseases leave you in a waiting room for healing that feels intolerable. Let me remind you today that the floor beneath these peaceless places is an unshakable foundation. May you be given the experience of peace, as you meditate on your unbreakable bond to the goodness and grace of God.

Oh Jesus, my necessary I AM, I cry out today in the horror of circumstance and in the hellishness of pain. My mind hurts. My body hurts. My soul throbs, and peace is so far out of reach. Would You bring to my mind today a fresh chapter of true, noble, pure, lovely, admirable, excellent, and praiseworthy things? Let me squeeze Your hand tightly and feel Your presence of peace, within, upon, and around me. I am worn out in sorrow. I am breaking under all that is crushing me. Oh, thank You Jesus that You are close, so very close to the brokenhearted and save the crushed in Spirit (Psalm 34:18, NIV). I am desperate and long to feel the fusion and the fruit of my heart bound to Yours. I surrender anxiety and ask that all my fragments and broken pieces would come back together under the power of Your peace and love.

CHAPTER TEN

I Am Hope

"We put our hope in the Lord. He is our help and our shield. In him our hearts rejoice, for we trust in his holy name. Let your unfailing love surround us, Lord, for our hope is in you alone."

Psalm 33:20–22, NLT

"While other worldviews lead us to sit in the midst of life's joys, foreseeing the coming sorrows, Christianity empowers its people to sit in the midst of this world's sorrows, tasting the coming joy."[24]

—Tim Keller

I t was a spring day that opened like an invitation, wooing me to live. It was March of 2000, my heartbroken year of college. I couldn't possibly shut myself inside a dark classroom where the tears could (and would) flow freely once again. The absence of my first love, Jeff, was like a bullet to the chest. My heart would certainly bleed out. This was grief. I needed to be in a place spacious enough and bright enough to usher me from dismal despair into wide-open hope.

I made a split-second decision to skip class and drove right past my parking spot. I had no idea where I was going as I weaved through downtown. Several minutes and turns later, I found myself

---

24 Keller, Timothy. *Walking with God Through Pain and Suffering.* Dutton, 2013, p. 29.

pulling through the massive wrought iron gates of the Lexington Cemetery. As I passed through the gates, it was like going back in time, entering an ancient kingdom harrowed by history. It was eerie, yet the sun reached through the clouds over this place of death, a spotlight to a stage which called my name.

This was the most luscious place of loss I'd ever seen. As I got out of my car and began walking through gardens, I sensed whatever lay before me was a role I was born to play. After several minutes, I came to an edge where the ground suddenly descended. Like the swooping train of a dress, the earth flowed into a Dale, a small circular valley of newborn grass speckled white with flowers. Awe swept over me, and I paused in wonder. Across the hill from me, a scattering of evergreens stood tall and protective. *How many tears have been shed here?* I surmised that rivers upon rivers of sorrow had been soaked up by these sturdy, shade-bearing soldiers.

I felt like a quarter getting ready to spiral down into one of those wishing funnels. What was my greatest wish? What was my desperate plea? I stood for a meditative moment, knowing I was the guest of honor to this sacred hour. The Holy Spirit had undoubtedly guided me to this Eden, to this perfect garden within death. I took a mesmerized breath, opened my eyes and heart wider, and took a step down the hill as the psalm came to mind:

> The Lord is my shepherd; I shall not want. He makes me lie down in green pastures. He leads me beside still waters. He restores my soul. He leads me in paths of righteousness for his name's sake. Even though I walk through the valley of the shadow of death, I will fear no evil, for you are with me; your rod and your staff they comfort me. (Psalm 23:1–4, ESV)

There was no doubt in my mind or heart at all that I *had* been led by an unseen but very real Shepherd. As I lay on the grass, a stage, my part to play became clear: I was *just* a sheep, and my only directive was dependence. It's nearly inexplicable to describe the hope that crept inside of me as I lay unfurled, looking at the sky. Every breath I took formed a deeper and wider space inside for hope to stretch out and make itself at home. Miraculously, a smile found my lips. *This is hope,* I thought. I was consumed by and enveloped with peace. I sat up, picked a few flowers (mementos), placed them in my journal, and wrote:

> *The difference between me and Eve in this garden I have discovered today is that I know my need for Jesus. I have the privilege in my pain of knowing I need a savior. But do I really know Him? Would I feel so alone or afraid if I did? As I sit here in the grass held in sunlight, it almost feels like a dream or a room in my heart. I was made to be in glory with Him, this place whispers of that....one day.*

An hour or so later, I closed my journal and walked beaming up the hill. I was still heartbroken by the loss of Jeff, yet I had been refreshed and restored by my Good Shepherd. I had just spent the morning with the Lover of my soul. I was nearly convinced that this miraculous morning wrapped around me like an invisible fortress. How could anything ever permeate or threaten this feeling, this hope, joy, and peace? Five years later, I entered the large wrought iron gates of the Lexington cemetery once more. This time, a mourning mother, waiting for her husband to place the box of our daughter's ashes in my hands. As I sat crying and waiting for Chris to come back to the car from the crematory, I looked ahead of me and suddenly remembered the last time I had been here. The irony struck me with pained confusion. Who was God to let this happen to me? Where was His fortress of protection now? Chris opened the door and placed death once again in my hands. The sobs unfurled into a new river to feed the trees. As we drove away, it seemed any remaining hope I had was left in the cemetery.

It would take years of grieving with God before I would understand and treasure both Him *and* the sovereign gift of hope that was my first trip to the cemetery. God knew then how my story would unfold. I would be at this graveyard again, with a more devastating loss, where the enemy would threaten me to believe hope was permanently gone. Satan would attempt to accuse and have me abandon the true Lover of my soul. Yet, that sacred moment in the Spring of my junior year of college was planted in a very sacred soil best described as "...eternity in the human heart..." (Ecclesiastes 3:11, NIV). We are born with a longing for perfection and companionship, the imprint of a map to the Way, the Truth, and the Life (John 14:6). The 23rd Psalm concludes with, "You prepare a table before me in the presence of my enemies. You anoint my head with oil; my cup overflows. Surely goodness and love will follow me all the days of my life, and I will dwell in the house of the Lord forever" (Psalm 23:5–6, NIV). *This* is hope, the confident assurance that I am followed with goodness, all while being led by goodness to glory. In trusting Him, our present thirst is served, and we know our ultimate thirst will be satisfied. I love how A.W. Tozer expresses God's nature unto ours: "God is so vastly wonderful, so utterly and completely delightful that He can, without anything other than Himself, meet and overflow the deepest demands of our total nature, mysterious and deep as that nature is."[25]

---

25 Tozer, A. W. *The Pursuit of God: The Human Thirst for the Divine.* Christian Publications, 2006. Chapter 1.

Before hope is an experience, hope is an instinct. We are hard-wired to cry, reach, trust, and depend. It is from this instinct to hope that we behave in a way for our hope to be met. Whether we realize it or not, we are constantly reaching with hope, for hope. We reach with the expectation that something or someone will ease the place of longing we were born with. We were created with the instinct to reach with hope's expectation of being held and satisfied by Father God. It's the nucleus of everything we are and who we will become. Hope is the fuel we run on as we drive through both good and grueling seasons until at last we are home and hope is no longer necessary. But until then, we reach. Longing is the arm extended from the capacity to hope, followed by the gift of hope; a measure given into the hand that is reaching. Experiencing hope comes by trusting and believing in the one and only God who fills us to overflowing with joy and peace (Romans 15:13). These fruits of the spirit (along with others) are treasures of hope placed into outstretched hands of dependent children.

Our intrinsic need to reach for God was made very real to me on a mission trip to Belarus with Chris the year before we got married. I had been to Minsk twice before. This was a first for Chris. I promised him he would fall in love with the people and culture just as I had. We had the unique opportunity to visit an orphanage for children with intellectual and physical disabilities. A small group of us, all women except for Chris, walked into a room housing babies with severe abnormalities. A precious boy, perhaps one year old, sat awkwardly in a crib. He had a severe protruding spinal malformation. As we walked up to the stoic baby, he looked at us and then zeroed in on Chris. A smile found his lips, and he reached for him. I was confused, and then I was in awe. This baby saw a man and found himself in a reaction of hope. He reached for a Father.

We were so excited for the next room of children. We brought gifts, stuffed animals, and toys from home to give to about thirty little ones with Down syndrome. I couldn't wait to see their faces light up as they received our fluffy and tangible love. We entered the room and opened huge bags of goodness. We felt like Santa's helpers. But once again, I was surprised and awed by the kids who ran and tackled Chris, swooning for his affection and joy while ignoring the toys. I watched in wonder. In both instances, the deepest demands of the total nature of these small, abandoned ones were a reaching and tackling hope for a Father. These experiences have stayed with me all my life. In the absence of everything, I witnessed hopeless orphans ignited with hope when presented with a kind, loving Father figure. They tapped into the nucleus of who they really are, sheep who know their only true want, The Shepherd. Oh, that I may realize I am the hurting child who needs her daddy to hold her, the orphan who would ignore the world's toys for the soul's truest demand for the Father.

This is our great hope here and now: that as we reach continuously for the God of hope, our strength will be renewed, we will mount up on wings like eagles, we will run and not be weary, we will walk and not faint (Isaiah 40:31). This is exactly what happened to me as a grieving college girl walking away from the cemetery. Joy and hope flowed out of me as I walked up the hill. My morning with God gave me exactly what I needed to keep on living... hope. Faith in my living, loving, pursuing Shepherd fanned the flame of my hope, my assurance of things unseen within, around, and before me (Hebrews 11:1).

As I keep reaching for God through many shadows of death, His goodness and mercy keep finding me. Strength, peace, and joy keep filling me, and hope's flame keeps lighting my way home.

I'll never forget the day I came to visit Krissy, and she was waiting for me at the door with a smile. I assumed she had good news, that our hope for shrinking cancer was on the tip of her tongue. Instead, she requested eagerly, "Katie, tell me everything you believe about heaven. Tell me everything the Bible has to say. Tell me all about what God has whispered to you of Anna. I want to know everything." She spoke like heaven was a place I'd visited, and she was getting ready to go there on vacation. There was so much joy and anticipation in her tone. She was overflowing with hope. I recognized it immediately, and I didn't like it one bit. I stared at her, warring within myself. Krissy's hope was shifting. Instead of looking behind her to the God who followed her with goodness, she was now looking ahead to the God who reached for her from heaven. She was scooting over her hope for miraculous healing to make room for her real and true home. She was running away from Earth's big bags of goodness, running toward her heavenly Father. But I wasn't ready to switch gears.

I let out the breath I'd been holding and replied, "Krissy, I don't want to talk about heaven with you. I don't want to have these conversations." The tears rolled down my cheeks. I couldn't embrace the thought of a world without Kristin.

But she gently coaxed me from the place where eternity beat strong in her heart, "You must tell me, Kate. Please tell me. Don't you want me to know what my home will be like?"

She knew I would do anything for her, even to push aside *my* hope for healing to make room for *her* hope for heaven. We sat and talked for hours. I shared the Biblical knowledge I had of heaven. I told her all the dreams and visions I'd had over the years of Anna twirling and dancing with Jesus in fields of flowers. I told her that the freedom I saw in Anna made me feel like I'd never lived at all.

I told her about the love and delight I saw in Jesus's eyes for her, a love I struggled but ached to experience myself. I told her that heaven was a place where we would meet God, our redeemer, in ways that would blow our minds, the exceedingly abundantly more of His imagination and creation. I told her about the God whom I believed would bring us into the great cloud of witnesses and allow us to be renewed in relationship to loved ones gone before us. I also told her I believed she would become a part of the great cloud for all of us who loved her so dearly (Hebrews 12:1–2).

Krissy was enraptured by my words. The Lord had given her a beautiful experience of being with Him in a garden at the beginning of her cancer journey. They stood forehead to forehead, embracing, and He whispered kindly and gently to her. I ended the conversation by telling her how much life she had to live and how she needed to keep fighting. She nodded, but I could tell that Krissy's hope for heaven was pounding. The nucleus of her soul was throbbing… she was coming alive even as her body was dying.

On my next visit to Charlottesville, I reluctantly handed Krissy a gift of hope—a memoir by a woman just like her: a beautiful wife, mother, and follower of Jesus battling cancer. Krissy's delicate fingers traced the words on the cover, and she read aloud, "*The Hardest Peace* by Kara Tippetts." She smiled at me and pulled the book into a hug. She was eager to read her words. As she climbed the stairs to her room to rest, I was appalled that I had just given her what felt like a bomb. Kara had just died.

Before I left that evening, I walked upstairs, hoping to press a quick kiss to Kristin's head. But as I opened the door, I found her sitting up, contemplative and serene, with the book pressed open on her lap. She turned to me and whispered, "Thank you. Thank you, Katie, for introducing me to my new friend. We will be friends soon, don't you think?" She was so calm and so at peace. Tears welled up in my eyes. I wanted to scream. I wanted to slap and punch and kick death in the face. I wanted to yell at the top of my lungs, "CANCER, YOU CAN'T HAVE HER!" But those words halted when her smile showed how eager she was for my reassuring response. I would not allow one argumentative word to escape my grieving heart. I smiled and answered her softly, "Of course you will be friends. She will love you as I do." She took a deep breath and smiled, rubbing my hand with her thumb as she had a thousand times before.

Some of Kara's words Kristin found refuge in that day were these: "He overcame my fear of death in that unbelievable, beautiful moment, and the fruit of that death, that resurrection, and that stunning grace is peace. It is the hardest peace, because it is brutal. Horribly brutal and ugly, and we want to look away, but it is the greatest, greatest story that ever was. And it was, and it is."[26]

The last sentence Kristin spoke to me in this world was to tell me she was going to heaven to enjoy a beautiful, perfect life with my daughter. "I'm going to take care of her for you, Kate," she said as she held my hand. I wept at the feel of our clasp and her words. I told her how I would always love her and asked her to tell Anna everything she could think to tell her, but mostly of my love. My Krissy was dying. My Krissy was being born. I was being emptied by sorrow and filled all the while with a mounting, overflowing kind of hope; a sadness followed with peace and joy.

On Jesus' final night with His twelve closest friends and followers, He sought to prepare them for His death. He tenderly called them His children and told them He would only be with them a

---

26 Tippetts, Kara. *The Hardest Peace: Expecting Grace in the Midst of Life's Hard.* David C. Cook, 2014.

little longer. He told them they couldn't follow Him, but that they would follow Him later (John 13:33–36). I can only imagine the sorrow and fear He saw in their faces as He delivered such sad and confusing news. But then He gave an elaborate gift of hope in John 14: "Let not your hearts be troubled."

Can you hear the tenderness and sympathy in His voice?

He continues, "Believe in God; believe also in me. In my Father's house are many rooms. If that were not so, would I have told you that I go to prepare a place for you? And if I go and prepare a place for you, I will come again and will take you to myself, that where I am you may be also" (John 14:1–3, ESV). "Truly, truly I say to you, you will weep and lament, but the world will rejoice. You will be sorrowful, but your sorrow will turn into joy" (John 16:20, ESV). "So also you have sorrow now, but I will see you again, and your hearts will rejoice, and no one will take joy from you" (John 16:22, ESV). Jesus is pleading with His boys to have hope. He is offering them a chance to see with the eyes of their hearts a snapshot of their eternal dwelling place. He knew that grief was about to overwhelm them. Hope was the only way they could move forward. The next time we see Jesus speak of heaven and offer hope is from the cross. To the repentant thief, Jesus declares, "Truly, I say to you, today you will be with me in paradise" (Luke 23:43, ESV). The word paradise comes from the Greek word *paradeisos,* which means a park. The root word *pardes* is of Persian origin and refers to a large enclosed garden of a king.[27] The garden was intended as a place of spiritual respite and a social space where the king would enjoy the company of friends.

---

27 Strong, James. *Strong's Exhaustive Concordance of the Bible.* Thomas Nelson, 1990. Entry G3857, H6508.

As I reflect on the dreams and visions God has given me over the years, I realize that the God of Hope gave me images of Paradise. Krissy had the same experience, and many others as well. I'll never forget the day my precious friend Beth (also Krissy's beloved cousin) visited from Georgia. She shared with us that as a friend of hers prayed for Kristin, the image came of a young girl holding onto the hem of Kristin's dress as they walked through fields of flowers. Beth said she knew instantly it was Anna. I AM, in His loving-kindness, gave us glimpses of glory to fuel our hearts with the joy and peace that come with the expectation of eternal salvation. I don't have to wonder what my girls are doing. They are enjoying life in the brightness of a perfect day amongst the beauty of a garden planted by the King to enjoy with the ones He loved and saved.

Consider the first garden ever planted: "Now the Lord God had planted a garden in the east, in Eden; and there he put the man he had formed. The Lord God made all kinds of trees grow out of the ground—trees that were pleasing to the eye and good for food. In the middle of the garden were the tree of life and the tree of the knowledge of good and evil" (Genesis 2:8–9, NIV). Eden literally means a place of pleasure.[28] God made man in His image and placed them in a luxurious, lush garden where He walked with them and loved them, and all felt immense pleasure.

We see similar words in Revelation: "Whoever has ears, let him hear what the Spirit says to the churches. To the one who is victorious, I will give the right to eat from the tree of life which is in the paradise of God" (Revelation 2:7, NIV).

---

28 Strong, James. *Strong's Exhaustive Concordance of the Bible*. Thomas Nelson, 1990. Entry H5731.

The Bible is *our* story. It is our beginning, middle, and end. From the first pages to the very last, we are shown the garden, the pleasure and beauty filled space where the Creator loves and enjoys His creation. This is the very reason why we do not grieve without hope: "Brothers and sisters, we do not want you to be uninformed about those who sleep in death, so that you do not grieve like the rest of mankind, who have no hope. For we believe that Jesus died and rose again, and so we believe that God will bring with Jesus those who have fallen asleep in him" (1 Thessalonians 4:13–14, NIV).

Our loved ones who died, who trusted Jesus as their way, truth, and life, are walking in the garden with Him. Our blueprint, our oldest memory, is Eden. Our present memories are lived in the Shepherd's Valley, and our future is Paradise. We were made for a beginning, middle, and end, that is the garden presence and provision of God.

I love Mark Buchanan's thoughts and words penned in his book *The Rest of God*. In his final chapter, "Practicing Heaven," he reflects,

> Jesus, speaking of things unseen, often talked about 'how much more.' 'If you, though evil, know how to give good gifts, how much more does your Father in heaven.' This last Sabbath liturgy is to help train your restless heart heavenward and it borrows from the logic of 'how much more.' If this meal with friends and family is rich, *how much more* the banquet of the great King? If resting in this patch of sunlight is refreshing, how *much more* to rest in that place where God and the lamb shine brighter than any sun. If lovemaking with my spouse is

blissful, how much more what no eye has seen, and no ear has heard but which God prepares for those He loves.[29]

I cannot grieve or grow in grace without reflecting on the assurances I have been given of things unseen. I want to multiply my hope through the discipline of paradise devotion, of "how much more" thinking and praising. I want my faith to be anchored in what will be revealed one day. I want my "now" to be dramatically and sacredly transformed by my meditation of "then." I want to cash in on my citizenship in heaven, to know that I am presently seated with Him in heavenly places and look back from paradise with the telescope that reveals my awful affliction as light and momentary. I *need* this faith. I want to listen and believe with the apostle John, as he heard a loud voice from the throne, saying:

> Behold, the dwelling place of God is with man. He will dwell with them, and they will be his people, and God Himself will be with them as their God. He will wipe away every tear from their eyes, and death shall be no more, neither shall there be mourning, nor crying, nor pain, for the former things have passed away. And he who was seated on the throne said, "Behold, I make all things new." (Revelation 21:3–5, ESV)

This is the greatest hope we have. We were made to dwell with God. What we have now is a "dwelling deposit" as intimate friendship with the Holy Spirit. But in Paradise, we will have Him face to face and hand in hand. Jesus will wipe every tear from our eyes, and we will never have to endure the grief of loss, life, or lies again.

---

29 Buchanan, Mark. *The Rest of God: Restoring Your Soul by Restoring Sabbath.* Thomas Nelson, 2006, pp. 214–15.

It all sounds good and true, but when we are enduring the awful and evil, it doesn't *feel* very good *or* true, does it? How do we get from hopeless to hopeful? What I can share with you is the practice that fans my hope to a flame within. As I visualize and meditate on Biblical hope realities, I go from empty to full. For me, Psalm 23 is the place to start.

I curl up in my bed, the one made with heavy layers of sadness and defeat. I close my eyes and imagine that I am curled up on the grass in the sunlight, which holds me warm in the cemetery. I am resting in green pastures by still waters. He sits with me as I rest and drink. *I am not alone.* I reach for Him just as the orphan boy reached for a Father. I invite my senses to come alive to this moment. What do I smell? *Honeysuckle, fresh air, budding grass.* What do I hear? *The slow roll of the stream, the song of the birds, the wind humming through the trees.* What do I feel? *The warmth of the sun against my face. The stroke of the Shepherd's hand anointing my head with oil.* The truth blooms from my soul and emerges to my lips: "I am just a sheep. All I want and need is my Shepherd." I breathe the words in and release them slowly. My brain, my body, and my spirit are all immersed in the psalm. Nothing has changed without, but so much is happening within. Instead of imagining my enemies and my fears, I begin to imagine Jesus setting a table with the most exquisite plates trimmed with gold and the most delectable spread of food. I see His delight in me as we look across the table at each other. The enemy's harassment becomes a mumble and then silence. Suddenly, my enemies and the lies don't matter. I am unafraid as I understand both the protection and passion coming from my Shepherd. I see all the pages of my life written. As Jesus thrums the pages, I am overwhelmed by all the highlighted sections, to the very last page. Each are moments of goodness and mercy already typed into time. My breath comes slow and easy. I open my eyes to reality, fully aware that a greater reality exists inside me and beyond me.

Another hope reality to ponder is Revelation 21:3–4. When grief consumes me, I insert myself into the greatest moment of comfort ahead. I close my eyes and imagine walking forward to see Jesus for the first time. I fall into Him, unable to stand as I weep all my life's tears all over again. A river of sadness surges through me. Jesus reaches for me and pulls me upright. He looks into my eyes with both gentleness and greatness. With His finger, He wipes the last tear I will ever shed. He smiles, and the empty reservoir from which my tears came is suddenly full and satisfied. Every question is answered. Every longing is met. Every wound is healed. Every grief is comforted. Every wrong vindicated. I take my first breath as a satisfied child of God, and Jesus whispers to me, "Behold, I have made everything new." Joyfully, He turns me around and points to the garden beyond. I see my girls, Anna, Violet, and Krissy, running through paradise for me.

This is how I fill my vessel of hope. I open my heart, mind, soul, and senses to the truest thing about me. I am a "hoper," made by hope, with hope, to experience hope until I am eventually satisfied and sanctified and never need to hope again. This is how I keep breathing and climbing back up the hills of despair to reenter my life. I imagine myself in the first garden as I imagine myself in the last. Hope is the presence of His life and love in the confines of our suffering. And hope is the reality of eternal life with God within the confines of death. We are renewed by hope when we think about all—the past, present, and future promises of Jesus fulfilled.

As I type the final words of this chapter, I imagine the many souls of suffering that will read these pages. I think upon your shadows of death and oceans of tears. My heart is pierced as I wonder about you. Can I invite you into God's Word with me, into the Garden of Eden? Into Psalm 23? Into heaven with your Comforter and Redeemer? This is the way to engage with eternity established within your heart. This is the way to ignite your hope and to know the love that surpasses knowledge and to be filled to the measure of all the fullness of God (Ephesians 3:19). Friend of suffering, may you find the courage to lament and long with a reaching trust for your Shepherd. May His spirit, His Word, and His heart be abundantly yours today.

Jesus, I am throbbing with sorrow. Just when I think I am all out of tears, they come again. I struggle with misery bound in this body, in this relationship, in this circumstance, in this grief. I am exhausted by this marathon of life and missing the ones I've lost. Jesus, I need hope! I beg You, sweep out my soul of anguish and deposit Your hope which leads to fountains of joy and peace. Let Your hope flow in me so continuously that I find myself caught up in hope moments throughout the day. Teach me to practice heaven, to be lifted and inspired by "how much more." Thank You, gentle and gracious I AM, for being the hope that rescues me day by day until hope is realized and fulfilled in Your forever kingdom. Pour out Your spirit upon me and open my eyes and ears as I read Your Word. By your spirit, take me deep into the reality that is greater than my life. Lead me to green pastures, still waters, and the table You have set for me today. Tell me the secrets of Your heart and give me glimpses of Your greatest glory.

CHAPTER ELEVEN

I Am Love

"I have loved you, my people, with an everlasting love.
With unfailing love, I have drawn you to myself."

Jeremiah 31:3, NLT

"Define yourself radically as one beloved by God. This is the true self.
Every other identity is illusion."[30]

—Brennan Manning

I was desperate to be with Chris. I hadn't seen him in two days, not since my sister had taken me to the hospital. The psychiatric floor allowed visitors every evening from 5–6 p.m. I stood in the doorway to my room and fixed my attention down the hall between the main entrance and the clock on the wall. It was almost 5:00 p.m. Both anxious and afraid, I didn't know what was happening to me, and I didn't know what would happen next. I felt like I'd lost my definition and was terrified that everyone I loved would be lost to me, especially Chris. How could he love me like this? I was an embarrassment and a disappointment. My shame was all-consuming. But the moment I saw Chris at the end of the hall, I saw the fire in his eyes for me, and I ran.

---

30   Manning, Brennan. *Abba's Child: The Cry of the Heart for Intimate Belonging*. NavPress, 2015, p. 42.

We lay in my bed and cried, holding each other. The last time we'd done this was after giving Anna to the nurse to be taken away from us forever. "I'm so sorry" and "Do you still love me" flowed freely with my tears. I wept relentlessly. Chris comforted, consoled, and reassured me. As the hour came to an end, He wrote on a piece of paper and handed it to me—*You are loved.* He explained, "I didn't write 'I love you' on purpose. It's so much bigger than that. You *are* loved, Kate." Chris was seeking to impress upon me that "Loved" is who I was, not just what he felt. He wanted me, in all my weakness, insecurity, and fear, to focus singularly on my truest identity. He was seeking to give me back my definition. Later that night, I wanted to talk to my sister. I reached the bedside table and opened the piece of paper she'd given me the night before. She had written down the phone numbers of my most important people since my cell phone had been taken away. My parents and siblings were at the top of the list, followed by Montica and Laura, my dearest friends from college, and Jess, my best friend in town. At the bottom of the paper in my sister's beautiful handwriting were the words, "You are so Loved." My breath caught, and I clutched the paper to my chest as I wept. There it was again… I was Loved. The next day, Jess came to visit. Without hesitation, she climbed into my bed and held my gaze. I was at once reassured by her love, and I fell apart in her arms. How often had she mothered me like this? Nurtured me right in the middle of my hard life? I expressed my great fear that I would lose her because of who I now was. How could she possibly still want to be my closest friend when I was such a mess? All the old, wicked lies that I was bad and dangerous came back with a force. Jess looked at me tenderly and said, "Nothing could ever keep me from loving you, Kate Kelty. It's you and me forever." Before she left, I asked her to write "You are Loved" on a piece of paper. She obliged, hugged me tight, and left. I felt entirely alone, except for my three "You are Loved" declarations from my dearest people. I clutched them to my heart and hoped the ink would seep deep inside. Why was it so hard for me to believe that I was loved? The idea of "lovable" has never been easy for me. I'd wrestled with self-hatred all my life. Though I confessed the love of God, I didn't realize the depths to which I had not yet received it. Because of His great love for me, living with partial awareness would never do. Like so many seasons before, like wayward Israel, the Lord allured me into the wilderness of mental health and spoke tenderly to me there. He gave me back my true worth, "You are Loved" and made the valley of trouble (the great suffering in my life) a doorway of hope (Hosea 2:15, NIV). One night during my hospitalization, I had a dream. I stood in the doorway of an exquisite bedroom. Everything was white. Two twin beds with abundant white blankets pooling to the floor were positioned on the back wall of the room. At the top of the unusually high ceilings, flowers painted gold crept down the wall from each corner, roses on one side, and violets on the other. Centered on the wall over the beds and stretching from one to the other, were three words penned in my cursive hand: *You Are Loved.*

I woke from the dream, and tears burst forth, wetting my cheeks with wonder. The Lord had just given me a glimpse of what could and might be the resting place of my girls and a deeper glimpse at the wonder of truest love. Now it was all beginning to make sense. I understood the inextinguishable love I held for my daughters. In fact, I knew nothing of them except love. I knew their value and worth were set apart from their conception. Not once had they done anything to prove their worth, and yet their value was immeasurable. "Loved" is who they were because their Heavenly Father dreamed them up and allowed Chris and me to conceive them. The Lord took what I held so unbelievably dear, the conviction of the value and treasure of my girls, to convince me of His love for me. *Kate, you are loved, just as Anna and Violet are loved.* Later that day, I sat by the window and stared at the vast rolling green hills. It almost looked like a painting made just for me. It reminded me of my hill at Massanetta. The words came, "I lift up my eyes to the hills. From where does my help come? My help comes from the Lord, who made heaven and earth" (Psalm 121:1–2, ESV). In that moment, my Helper and Maker opened the eyes of my heart, and an image flashed before me. I saw Jesus take a small glowing ball of light from His heart, and He placed it within my mother's womb. It was so small and sudden, but light-ning power accompanied it. God loved me, delighted in me even before my conception. A shaking in my heart began. An earth-quake was coming. The foundation of my soul cracked open, and I knew it as wide as the ocean and tall as the heavens: *I am Loved.*

This time, I didn't just contemplate the phrase; the phrase contemplated me. Instead of accessing the truth and finding bro-ken places where it might fit, the truth rushed in and filled every crack and cranny of my disbelief. I felt sad for the forty-one years it had been so difficult to believe and thrilled for the years that re-mained to relish in the reality. I was loved because I was made and sustained by my loving Father.

To be fully transformed and freed by the love of God, we must go back to the beginning, to the very first page of our story: "Then God said, 'Let *Us* make mankind in *Our* image…'" (Gen-esis 1:26, NIV; emphasis added). There is enormous love in this verse, though the word "love" is never mentioned. We were made by an "Us." We weren't just created; we were spiritually conceived. The most intimate and perfect of all relationships caused the birth of mankind. Our arrival as image bearers of the Trinity, the Sovereign, the Savior, and the Spirit, was a celebrated manifestation of their deepest love and desire.

Years ago, I heard someone say, "Man was born out of the laughter of the Trinity." I remember thinking, *wouldn't it be wonderful if that were true?* A lovely thought, but way too intimate and emotional for the God I imagined. Holiness couldn't be so human, could it? I was gravely mistaken. If there is any confusion or guessing about what emotions were present for God the Father, God the Son, and God the Spirit at creation, Proverbs 8 gives us the answer. King Solomon allows "wisdom" to speak:

> I was there when He set the heavens in place,
>
> when He marked out the horizon on the face of the deep,
>
> when He established the clouds above
>
> and fixed securely the fountains of the deep,
> when He gave the sea its boundary
>
> so the waters would not overstep His command,
> and when He marked out the foundations of the earth.
>
> Then I was constantly at His side.
>
> I was filled with delight day after day,
>
> rejoicing always in His presence,
>
> rejoicing in His whole world
> and delighting in mankind.
>
> (Proverbs 8:27–31, NLT)

This "voice of wisdom" is the personification of Jesus. He invites us into His giddy and glorious feelings and reactions as Father God, *Yahweh*, created us. He wants us to know that *He* was constantly at *His* side. There is no distance between Father and Son. They are inseparable. Their actions and reactions are essential to each other. Secondly, Jesus rejoices in God's presence and rejoices and delights in the world and mankind. The Hebrew word for rejoicing in this passage is śāhaq, which means to laugh and play with pleasure; to have fun.[31] Can you see the glee, the belly laughs, and playfulness of Jesus when we were made? Can you pause for a moment and visualize Jesus delighting and laughing at the unique wonder of you?

I can't help but picture the look on Chris's face when Anna was born. Though she lay dead in my arms, he smiled and chuckled at the unique beauty of our daughter revealed, a daughter made in *our* image. This daddy couldn't be held back from joy, not even when death had robbed him. I can also picture the way Chris teases, laughs, and plays with our living children. Fathers are hardwired for delighted play with their image bearers… our God is no different. I thought laughter was too human of an emotion to ascribe to God, when all along, laughter and rejoicing are traits we receive from Him. Expressions lavished on us at our divine conception. Yes, we were born out of the laughter of the Trinity, and we were created by love.

> For you created my inmost being;
>
> you knit me together in my mother's womb.
>
> I praise you because I am fearfully and wonderfully made;
>
> your works are wonderful,
>
> I know that full well.

---

31 Strong, James. *Strong's Exhaustive Concordance of the Bible*. Thomas Nelson, 1990. Entry H7832.

My frame was not hidden from you

when I was made in the secret place,

when I was woven together in the depths of the
earth.

Your eyes saw my unformed body;

all the days ordained for me

were written in your book

before one of them came to be.

How precious to me are your thoughts, God!

How vast is the sum of them!

Were I to count them,

they would outnumber the grains of sand—

When I awake, I am still with you.

(Psalm 139:13–18, NIV).

I wish I had understood as a self-loathing child, an anorexic teenager, and a depressed and grieving young mother that I was wonderfully made. I often repeated the words in desperation, but the truth struggled to permeate the wall of false beliefs around my heart. I was certainly *not* wonderful; I was convinced of that. I had a long list of all the reasons why I was awful and wretched, and shame delighted in reading it to me frequently.

"Wonderfully made" refers to how and why we were created, not what we become. My "wonderful" was the unique way I was divinely imagined and distinguished from before my conception. God knew me and set me apart before I was yet conceived (Jeremiah 1:5). When I was still a thought in the mind of a perfect Creator, I was wonder-*full*. This reminded me of the image Jesus gave me in the hospital of being a ball of light taken from His heart and placed within my mother. We are taken from His very soul, the place where His truest delights dwell, and given life. Now two definitions claim me: I am Loved and *I am wonderful.* To be loved and to be wonderful are the threads by which God fashions His children. In Psalm 139:13, when David describes the manner in which we were created, he uses the word "formed," meaning to create, buy, purchase, acquire, and redeem. David is literally saying, "You *purchased* and *redeemed* my inmost being, and I am fearfully and wonderfully made." God's mercy and our need for it were stitched into every inch of our souls. His mercy wasn't a reaction to our sin; rather, His mercy preceded our sin. When God reached His hands into the earth of Eden to form Adam, He knew He would plunge the very depths of the earth to save him. When Jesus laughed and played with His children in the garden before sin claimed the world, He knew that only by His shed blood would they be permitted to enter the paradise garden of heaven. He knew it all and formed us anyway. In fact, being fearfully (in awe of God) and wonderfully made (set-apart and distinguished) is the imprint of redemption on our souls. We were created to be claimed by the cross.

I love the way the redeeming love of Jesus is expressed in Romans chapter five: "Very rarely will anyone die for a righteous person, though for a good person someone might possibly dare to die. But God demonstrates his love for us in this: While we were still sinners, Christ died for us" (Romans 5:7–8, NIV).

Paul magnifies the magnificence and uniqueness of God's love, given to us when we least deserved it. He gave His perfect life for sinners. King David grasped this centuries before in Ephesians 1:5—that "God decided in advance to adopt us into His own family by bringing us to Himself in Jesus Christ. This is what He wanted to do, and it gave Him great pleasure" (NLT). God's desire to rescue us was so abundant that it gave Him pleasure greater than His grief. His love for the whole world was so immense that He sacrificed His one and only to save all (John 3:16). I am convinced there is no greater love to be found! But can it withstand anything? I am harassed by the fear that at some point, His pleasure will run out, and love will no longer come for me. I recall that Paul asked the same question:

> Can anything ever separate us from Christ's love? Does it mean He no longer loves us if we have trouble or calamity, or are persecuted, or hungry, or destitute, or in danger, or threatened with death? ... No, despite all these things, overwhelming victory is ours through Christ, who loved us. And I am convinced that nothing can ever separate us from God's love. Neither death nor life, neither angels nor demons, neither our fears for today nor our worries about tomorrow— not even the powers of hell can separate us from God's love. No power in the sky above or in the earth below—indeed, nothing in all creation will ever be able to separate us from the love of God that is revealed in Christ Jesus our Lord. (Romans 8:35, 37–39, NLT)

The love of God is a flawless force that made us, saved us, and can *never* fail us. In the months following my hospitalization, God's perfect love began driving away the deep fear that I could damage others and God and thwart their love toward me. The beloved disciple's words rang deep and true: "There is no fear in love. But perfect love drives out fear, because fear has to do with punishment. The one who fears is not made perfect in love" (1 John 4:18, NIV). I don't think I realized how unsafe I'd felt until the fear of punishment was gone. Love drove it out, and grace took its place. Now a third definition claims me: I am loved, I am wonderful, and *I am secure.*

The love of Christ cemented me in the warm reality that though I have been and will be shaken and broken by loss, life, and lies, I can never be disconnected from the gripping and permanent love of Christ Jesus. This love celebrates me. This love rescues me. This love heals and blesses me, and this love is perfect. I can always count on the flawless love of Jesus.

Anna, Johnny, Benjamin, Elijah Drew, Jones, Vivi Joy, and Violet are each resting in the reality that they are the beloved of God. They are my loves, and I have the immeasurable pleasure of being their mama. Each is fearfully and wonderfully made, and each was formed by a redeeming hand and an unrelenting heart. I have never felt more like myself than when my babies have nestled sleeping against my chest. Perhaps that's because it's the closest I will ever get to reflecting the father heart of God; a parent delighting in His dependent child. How many months and years has that rocking chair been my home? Back and forth, I rocked crying babies in the rhythm of unconditional love.

I've been rocked, too. Jesus carried me to the hospital, placed me on His lap, and rocked me into a new reality. This room for the sick was a nursery to God. In the space of seven days, He *formed* something entirely new in me. He hushed the world and my warring mind, and when all was quiet, I could finally hear what he'd been singing over me all along: *Kate, You Are So Loved.*

Paul's prayer to the Ephesians both anchors and guides me now as I live on toward paradise: "And may you have the power to understand, as all God's people should, how wide, how long, how high, and how deep his love is. May you experience the love of Christ, though it is too great to understand fully. Then you will be made complete with all the fullness of life and power that comes from God" (Ephesians 3:18–19, NLT).

We live in a world and in relationships where not understanding, believing in, and counting on the perfect love of God is soul-crushing. Our wounds, needs, and the demands of our lives are too great to withhold ourselves from the true nature of His love and our existence for it. We weep in the loneliness of singleness and broken marriage. We ache from the places where our parents made us feel we were not enough and that we had to be a certain way to obtain their love and acceptance. We cry in the cavernous spaces left by spouses who died, and the "I love you's" we no longer get to hear. We wrestle with the pain of our own self-loathing and the fear that deep down, if people really knew us, they would take their love away. Those closest to us hurt us, abandon us, and break us. We must know and rely on the perfect love of Jesus, or we will never reach the heights and depths of the pleasure and peace that love was intended to give.

I breathe deep and whisper on an inhale, "I am." I hold at the top of the breath, slowly release, and then declare "loved." Repeatedly, I breathe the truth: I AM loves me…I am Loved! All the parts of me that feel unaccepted are disassembled. All the parts in me that feel unwanted are desired. All the parts in me that feel embarrassed are excused. All the parts in me that hurt from lesser loves are unhooked. All the parts in me that ache from loneliness are filled and flooded. He is unlike us. He doesn't give His heart in pieces. He doesn't give a spoonful here and there. He doesn't give good love today and bad love tomorrow. He gives it all, perfectly, all the time. Yes, we were made in love. We were saved by Love. We are purposed for love. And by Him, we can assuredly speak of ourselves, *I am Loved. I am wonderful and I am secure.*

I AM is ours, and *we* are His.

I can imagine the throbbing ache and the tears that may be falling as you read the words, "You are loved." But the enemy wants nothing more than for you to believe the opposite. Can you stop for a moment and just breathe? Speak "I am" and inhale deeply. Hold the breath and then release it slowly. When the breath runs out, declare "loved." Please stop reading. Breathe deeply into the truest reality about yourself for several breaths.

Beloved. You were created with pleasure and delight. You were made to be rescued and redeemed. Every pain in your heart, ailment in your body, and brokenness in your life can be redeemed by the truth that *you are loved.*

Jesus, thank You for making me in love and for love. Thank You that I am fearfully and wonderfully made. Thank You that because of the cross, I am secure. Take me back to the beginning, to the moment when I was only a smile in Your heart and light in Your hand. Help me to know and believe that this very moment, You sing a song of deliverance over me. Consume me with the truth that You delight in me and that just a single thought of me gives You great pleasure. Rock me in this moment to stillness. Hush the worries and fears in my heart and let me respond to Your love with dependence upon it.

CHAPTER TWELVE

I Am Forgiveness

*"For His unfailing love toward those who fear Him
is as great as the height of the heavens above the earth.
He has removed our sins as far from us
as the east is from the west."*

Psalm 103:11–12, NLT

"To forgive is to set a prisoner free and to discover that the prisoner was you."[32]

—Lewis B. Smedes

I tripped on the not-so-distant memory. The barely mended gash in my heart ripped open once again. Every time I thought of him, this happened—a sting—a gush—and then the nausea, anger, and disgust. I was forty years old and in an unhealthy relationship that shocked me like an avalanche. How could the man who helped me heal from trauma cause new trauma? I had dismissed the red flags and uncomfortable moments because I trusted his character and was grateful for his professional and spiritual help. However, there came a point in time when I knew I could never see him for help or hurt again.

---

32 Smedes, Lewis B. *Forgive and Forget: Healing the Hurts We Don't Deserve.* HarperCollins, 1984.

It took time to trust a new counselor with my story, but when I did, the ball of truth—and therefore healing—began to roll. Dana filed two separate reports against this man, but when he was confronted by the state medical board, as well as a phone call from Dana, he shifted blame and used my client status against me. I was once again "unsafe and dangerous." He peeled blame and shame like stickers and unfairly placed those scarlet letters all over me. I was exhausted by holding the pain of this unfair and damaging season in my life. I wanted to throw the ticking bomb of hurt and anger as far away from me as possible, but I was stuck. From previous healing with past abusers, I knew that unforgiveness is like leaving a broken piece of shrapnel embedded in the skin. I wanted to forgive, to completely remove the offense and offender from within me, but somehow letting go felt worse than holding on. Why did this feel like handing him my heart? Why did this feel like condoning his sin? Why did offering forgiveness feel like being violated all over again?

I don't have to wonder if you know what I'm talking about. We have all been hurt in relationships. Some of that hurt was intentional, some was not. Some of it was careless and some was cruel. Some intentional and some accidental. Some of the pain was inflicted by healthy people we love, and some by unhealthy people we love. Some of the pain is inflicted by spiritual leaders—even heroes. When the person who hurts you is able to hear, process, and humbly offer an apology, an easy road of forgiveness, healing, and restoration is paved out before us. But what about the offender who stares at you like you're crazy and tells you your pain is your problem, your fault? Have you experienced this disorienting and unfair tactic of blame shifting or gaslighting? The kind of response that makes you question your sanity and keeps thrusting you into a cyclone of confusion?

I am sad to say I have sat with too many who have been slapped and marred by psychological, emotional, spiritual, sexual, relational, parental, and marital abuse. If you just read those words and the deepest place in your heart is now throbbing, let me pause and create sacred space to say to you... *I am so sorry.* You didn't deserve it. Even your sin does not justify the mistreatment and abuse of another. What happened to you is not okay. Yahweh knows and Yahweh grieves for you. Yahweh also has an exit to release you from the pain that traps your hurt, anger, and disgust. That exit is forgiveness.

The enemy lies to us about what forgiveness is and isn't. He places caution tape and warning signs at the cell doors that hold us as prisoners of pain. But it's a trick. The devil's way of keeping us "safe" is to keep us bound in bitterness. The key to freedom is walking out of the cell and walking through the door of forgiveness, as excruciating as it may be. Offering forgiveness is especially painful when an offender has not acknowledged or repented of their offenses or presumes to be the greater victim. How do we forgive when trauma is lodged in our brains, bodies, and souls? How do we forgive when our memories, beliefs, and daily lives hold reminders of the wrong done to us? How do we forgive when another's sin has mottled our minds and morphed our lives?

"Get rid of all bitterness, rage and anger, brawling and slander, along with every form of malice. Be kind and compassionate to one another, forgiving each other, just as in Christ God forgave you" (Ephesians 4:31–32, NIV). These instructions are listed so quickly that it could read like a bullet-point to-do list: *take out the trash, bring in the groceries.* But it's not that simple. The word forgive (*nâsâ'*) means to lift up, to bear up, or to carry.[33] When we forgive, we are lifting up and even bearing another's sin. I love how Tim Keller expresses this in his book, *Forgive: Why Should I and How Can I?*, "Forgiveness, then, is a form of voluntary suffering. In forgiving, rather than retaliating, you make a choice to bear the cost."[34] Imagine that the unforgiven sin of another, along with unhealed trauma, inhabits your heart like an old, rotting sofa that weighs a ton and interferes with everything. It needs to be hauled away, but it shouldn't be your responsibility. That hard and hefty task belongs to the one who moved it in and left it there to overwhelm your heart. Of course, this makes sense, and yet some of the heaviest, most heinous couches don't move an inch without our blood, sweat, and tears. We want the offender to remember what he/she did, knock on our door, and grovel on bended knees: "I am so sorry I left that heinous piece of sin and trauma in your way. Please forgive me and let me get it out of here as quickly as possible." Such a lovely script, yet it is so rarely repeated to those who most deserve and are desperate for it.

Is there a way to heal without forgiveness? Can we take every healthy step forward except to forgive and be well? Will ignoring it ease the pain? Will cursing it make the couch shrink? Is there anything we can do or say apart from bearing the weight of another's "sin" and moving it ourselves? "For while we were still weak, at the right time Christ died for the ungodly" (Romans 5:6, ESV). Jesus took every massive, rotting sin of man upon Himself, so that we could thrive in souls free of obstruction and filled with the most quality furnishings: love, joy, peace, patience, kindness, goodness,

---

33   Strong, James. *Strong's Exhaustive Concordance of the Bible*. Thomas Nelson, 1990. Entry H5377.

34   Keller, Timothy. *Forgive: Why Should I and How Can I?* Viking, 2022, p. 189.

faithfulness, gentleness, and self-control (Galatians 5:22–23). This is the example of how God wants us to operate in relationships: to forgive, *the same way He* forgave us.

I first came to process the generosity of God's forgiving nature on a harrowing visit to a concentration camp in Poland. It was the summer of 1999, after my sophomore year in college. I traveled with a group from my campus ministry to Minsk, Belarus, for ten weeks. We had just finished reading *The Hiding Place* by Corrie Ten Boom. We all felt so connected to her horror and her heart. We were inspired by her. We were timid but ready for the mid-summer trip to Auschwitz-Birkenau.

All my camera film from that trip got ruined, but the images are forever burned in my mind. The long train track that brought us into the camp, the same one from the movie "Auschwitz." The gas chambers and shooting posts in the courtyard, the mounds upon mounds of black shoes, wire spectacles, human hair, ashes, and clothing—it was heinous to behold. Our Polish guide told stories that left us all feeling sick and horrified. The moment most memorable and haunting to me happened in "Block 11." Outside of the gas chambers, this is where most punishment took place. We were invited to go into a "standing cell." I was so brave then. I didn't want to miss a moment to feel or experience anything.

These cells were four spaces, each measuring less than one square meter. The only source of air was a five-by-five centimeter opening covered with a metal grille. To stand in the cell, you had to crawl through a small opening on the floor, which was closed with bars and a wooden hatch. Four prisoners were confined in each of these spaces for anywhere from one to twenty nights, forced to work the next day. Within seconds of being pressed up against three others with no light and no room to breathe, I felt suffocated and terrified. I started shaking. I imagined the smells, the excrement, the fear. I wanted to get out. I *needed* to get out. I can't write about the experience without feeling it all over again in my body. I have struggled with claustrophobia ever since. When we left the standing cell, we stood in a typical cell. I began to cry as I stared at etchings and inscriptions of prisoners on the walls—desperate pleas, prayers, and goodbyes. It was too horrific. Too real. The heaviest sorrow, deepest anguish, and the hottest anger were searing me from the inside out. This place was hell on earth, and every evil guard was an employee of the devil himself. Here I was, feeling all this wretched emotion, and yet the evil from this war had not personally affected me. My rage was a magnet. I felt as though I was pulled and smashed in between those guards in the standing cell. I hated them for their cruelty, and that hatred bound me to them. How did Corrie manage it, I wondered? How did she break free from hate?

After the war, Corrie traveled and spoke to many with God's message of forgiveness. In these messages, she would share the imagery that confessed sin was thrown into the deepest ocean by God. On one such afternoon, she was approached by a man she recognized instantly as a guard from the camp she and her sister had been taken to—the one where her sister slowly died. This was a first for her. She had never stared into the face of one of her offenders before.

"A fine message, *fräulein!*" (a young, unmarried German woman), he told her. He proceeded to share how thankful he was to know his sins were at the bottom of the sea. He reached out his hand to her. At the sight of his hand, Corrie fumbled in her pocketbook. She felt her blood freeze. How could she take this man's hand?

"You mentioned Ravensbrück in your talk. I was a guard there. But since that time, I have become a Christian. I know that God has forgiven me for the cruel things I did there, but I would like to hear it from your lips as well. *Fräulein*, will you forgive me?"

He extended his hand once more. Corrie recalls,

> I stood there with the coldness clutching my heart… forgiveness is an act of the will, and the will can function regardless of the temperature of the heart. 'Jesus, help me!' I prayed silently. 'I can lift my hand. I can do that much. You supply the feeling.' And so woodenly, mechanically, I thrust my hand into the one stretched out to me. And as I did, an incredible thing took place. The current started in my shoulder, raced down my arm, sprang into our joined hands. And then this healing warmth seemed to flood my whole being, bringing tears to my eyes. 'I forgive you, brother!' I cried. 'With all my heart!' For a long moment, we grasped each other's hands, the former guard and the former prisoner. I had never known God's love so intensely as I did then.[35]

As I think of this moment for Corrie and the forgiven guard-turned-brother, I imagine them crawling out of the standing cell together. I see them walking into the light of day and can hear the cascade of waves crashing at the ocean's edge. Their sin was gone, buried deep in the sea. Freedom was gifted to them both.

I will never forget the moment I sat with Dana and finally expressed aloud all the pain I felt from my unapologetic and accusing

---

35 Boom, Corrie, et al. *The Hiding Place*. Bantam, 1971, p. 238.

offender. I described every gross and confusing encounter of being both helped and hurt by him. And when I was done, I covered my face, curled up on her couch, and wept. But then an unbelievable thing happened. I had a deep knowing that Jesus was weeping, too. He wasn't mad at me because I was struggling to forgive; He was heartbroken at the way I'd been hurt by one of His wounded and unrepentant sons. As Dana poured out her apology on behalf of the profession and allowed me to hear and understand her own sadness and anger over the ways I had been mistreated, I started to relax in her words… which *were* the truth. And then it dawned on me that the *truth* is the only thing needed to move forward. The truth is what we need for freedom (John 8:32). I didn't *need* an apology from my "brother" because I had heartfelt remorse from *our* Dad.

Friend of suffering, you may never get an "I'm sorry" from your offender. You may never get the validation or recompense your violation deserves. You may never get the closure of being heard and believed, but you certainly do have a grieved and heart-sick apology from your Heavenly Father.

We can't have it both ways. We can't love and cherish the forgiveness that reaches from the cross and rescues us from the quick-sand of *our* sin while holding and pressing down another "sibling" to be swallowed by theirs. God has so much more for our hearts and hands to do in the abundant life He promises that can't be accessed or lived if we are stuck in the standing cells of unforgiveness.

When I struggle to forgive, I meditate on the merciful judgment of our all-powerful God. There is a future moment when every person on this earth will be called up from our "rooms" to stand before our Dad and King. It won't be a conversation, because there will be nothing to explain or defend. We will see and hear every one of our deeds, words, and motives laid out. When we see it the way He sees it, we will grieve for how we've grieved Him and each other. We will weep at Jesus' feet, and I imagine we will want a do-over, a chance to forgive as He forgives and to love as He loves. We will ache for one more chance to live fully into the abundance He died, forgave, and redeemed us to live.

I also ponder the reality that when every son and daughter stands before the throne of judgment, no matter the weight or sum of our sins, the punishment is the same for us all. One drop of deadly poison isn't less harmful than a thousand—it all yields the same result: death. Yet, here is the Great News of our Great God and the final key we graciously receive when we are adopted as His children: HE DIED FOR US ALL. He died for His precious, obedient mother, and every sinful soul that whipped, cursed, spat upon, and nailed Him to the cross. He stood in the standing cell of hell, pressed up against the devil himself, so we wouldn't have to. Upon salvation, we receive the key to unlock the cells of our sin, and that same key offers the power to forgive. Let's not live our lives pressed up against the sin of another, prevented from living the abundant life His resurrection power fully offers. This may be revelatory and motivating to pursue forgiveness, but how do we actually do it when we are still feeling the very traumatizing effects of the pain inflicted by another?

One of the tools Dana gave me was the insight that our brains don't easily differentiate between the imaginary and real. A fake conversation can yield a whole lot of healing. Since I knew it wouldn't be healthy or beneficial to talk to the person who was denying my experience with him, I wrote a letter identifying everything that wounded me and read it out loud in the safety of my home. It was as if I was saying, "I am so hurt that I trusted you as a professional 'mover' to help haul away my old heavy trauma. And all the while, you were dropping off new pieces of your sin for me to trip over and to be infected by. My heart houses new trauma because of you." When all of that was emptied out, I wrote, "Now I want to forgive you, to remove the clutter and chaos of your sin, not because you've asked for it, but because I want to love and honor God and you, my spiritual sibling. I am powerless to lift this, except that Christ's forgiving nature is within me. By faith and trust in the power that raised Jesus from the dead, I lift your sin, I carry it even, and move it out of my heart and to the foot of the cross. I don't want to miss one fraction of the abundant life God has planned for me."

As I finished reading, tears spilled from my eyes, and an image came to my mind. I was connected to this man, heart to heart, by a long and heavy rope. It was pulled tight between us, and I realized without cutting it, without forgiveness, I would never be free. I imagined cutting the rope, and I flew back into the arms of Jesus.

And then the most incredible thing happened. When I looked back at the offender, he was just a boy. He was no longer big enough to cast a shadow over me. He was scared and wounded. He was alone and crying. I was struck with compassion for him. I saw that the hurt he inflicted and the blame he shifted to me were rooted in fear. The lies he believed, the love he didn't know, and the pride that entangled him kept him enslaved. The resurrection power of God within me was stirred by holy compassion. But instead of that empathy making me feel responsible for him, I found myself praying for Jesus to release him from every cell his sin, shame, and fear had locked him in. It felt right to trust Jesus with the consequences of his choices and his restoration story. It felt good to let God be Judge and Father for this broken brother of mine.

I felt liberated for the first time in months. My lack of forgiveness, the way I nursed my anger and hurt, and endless rumination kept me pressed up against my offender in the dark and tight cell of *his* sin. I was so scared that forgiveness would let him off the hook, when really, forgiveness let me off the hook and out of his standing cell. Forgiveness gives. We are so frightened it will rob us of something we need to hold onto to be okay, but in forgiving, we are given new space, new mercy, and new love and compassion from our Father.

In the weeks that followed, I learned that forgiveness isn't a one-and-done. Forgiveness doesn't mean our trauma disappears. I often get hit by triggers that cause the "arthritis" of my trauma to flare. At first, I was discouraged that this meant I had not truly forgiven. Now I understand that as long as I live in this body, which keeps the score of my earthly story, old wounds can throb and even split open once again. This can either be an invitation to discouragement or joy. We can feel deflated by our "lack of progress" or rejoice that God is allowing another moment for us to do as He did on the cross.

I love Paul's heart cry in His letter to the Philippians: "I want to know Christ—yes, to know the power of His resurrection and participation in his sufferings, becoming like him in his death, and so, somehow, attaining to the resurrection from the dead" (Philippians 3:10–11, NIV).Every moment we *get* to forgive is a moment we *get* to take laps in the pool of God's cleansing grace and to extend the same invitation to another. We can offer it by faith (not feeling) and know we are seeking to take up our cross as He did. When Jesus died for our sins, He didn't feel ready or wanting for it. He begged His Father while sweating blood, "Father, if you are willing, please take this cup of suffering away from me." But in faith and trust, He yields, "Yet I want your will to be done, not mine" (Luke 22:42, NLT).

Jesus shows us how faith trumps feelings when it comes to forgiveness. How did He do it? How did He press through excruciating murder to pave the way for us to be forgiven and rejoined with God? "...For the joy set before Him he endured the cross..." (Hebrews 12:2, NIV). Can we harness the same joy? Can we so esteem the beauty of becoming more like Him that we can press through the pain of forgiveness, knowing joy greater than our pain, bitterness, anger, and hurt awaits? King David pens this truth so beautifully in Psalm 32:

> Oh, what joy for those
> whose disobedience is forgiven,
> whose sin is put out of sight!
> Yes, what joy for those
> whose record the LORD has cleared of guilt,
> whose lives are lived in complete honesty!
> When I refused to confess my sin,
> my body wasted away, and I groaned all day long.
> Day and night your hand of discipline was heavy on me.
> My strength evaporated like water in the summer heat.
> Finally, I confessed all my sins to you
> and stopped trying to hide my guilt.
> I said to myself, "I will confess my rebellion to the LORD."
> And you forgave me! All my guilt is gone.
> (Psalm 32:1–5, NLT)

What about if the sin done to you was so evil that it has permanently marred your life? A drunk driver killed a loved one. A rape that cost you everything. Hidden abuse that has psychologically and emotionally shredded you? A lie that destroyed your life and robbed you of both your financial security and reputation. A deceptive narrative spoken and spread that has sullied your name, scattered friends, and stabbed your soul? When we can say with all honesty and humility, "Lord, it feels impossible to forgive this person who tortured me, but please help me, I don't want to be imprisoned by this," He will honor that prayer and guide us forward to forgive. He is our advocate. He is presently praying for us all. That prayer certainly includes His desire for us to forgive one another. Sometimes, He asks us to trust Him to forgive when our feelings don't change. And sometimes, like Corrie, we extend our hands to our enemies and find Jesus' love and feelings surging through us. One way to harness this love is by obeying what Jesus encouraged His disciples to do in Matthew 4: "But I say to you, Love your enemies and pray for those who persecute you, so that you may be sons of your Father who is in heaven. For he makes his sun rise on the evil and on the good, and sends rain on the just and on the unjust" (Matthew 5:44–47, ESV).

This takes forgiveness to a new and higher level. From forgiving to just *giving*. This is a blessing! And why exactly does God want us to do this? To be like Him. We look most like our Daddy when we love those who sin against us. My friend Christine is beautiful at being like her heavenly Father in this way. When Christine is aware of the pain or hurt she feels from another, she asks the Lord to show her His unique heart of love for them. The Holy Spirit undeniably speaks to her, and she begins praying, blessing, and honoring that soul. Sometimes it's just between her and the Lord. Sometimes she writes letters and sends corresponding gifts.

She takes very seriously her desire to be a daughter who reflects the love of her Daddy. I was blown away when she first shared this with me. I told her about a conversation with someone where I felt justifiably hurt. I was considering a "truth in love" conversation. My sweet friend looked at me with such compassion. She validated my hurt, and then she encouraged me to "be the light" instead of "shedding the light." She basically told me to speak blessing to the *wounded* part of this person, and not the wound-*ing* part. It was both revelatory and transformational for me.

I recognize what a loaded chapter this is. In fact, just the thought of the collective pain being pricked and stirred for you is causing my chest to pound and my eyes to water. Please know how deeply and desperately sorry I am for every unfair and wrong thing that has ever been done to you. I am sorry for the ways you have felt pushed into a standing cell and for the ways you can't seem to get out. My greatest longing is that you could empty your soul to Jesus, the Great I AM, and imagine His deepest anguish and most sincere apology to you. This is where the healing begins. I hope and pray that you find safe others to begin the journey of opening your soul to. Someone who knows the heart of God and your heart and can lead you gently into a healing process. And I hope and pray that whatever false beliefs you hold about what forgiveness is and isn't would be shattered.

Maybe your heart is throbbing for another reason. Is the Spirit inviting you to look at a part of yourself you've been unwilling to see? Have you hurt others from unhealed places? Have you dropped off heavy and even abusive words or treatment in another's heart? It's not too late to ask the Lord for forgiveness. It's not too late for remorse for the one you harmed. This may or may not bring about reconciliation, but repentance will give the healing and freedom you desperately need. The hardest and yet holiest place you can be is on the floor in humility, lavished by the perfect love of God. Be brave and let the lock of pride fall away. Be freed from the standing cell of your sin.

May we all who know the punctures of hurting and being hurt, be eased, comforted, and soothed by the God who paved the way to freedom and abundance by His excruciating entrance and powerful exit of the standing cell.

Jesus, I am sick with hurt. I don't even know how to parse it all out or how to begin talking with You about it. Thank You that my groans make sense to You. "Before a word is on my tongue you, Lord, know it completely." (Psalm 139:4, NIV). Thank You that my wounds and abrasions are known to You. I have Your empathy and Your remorse and Your deep condolence for what happened to me in plain sight and in secret. Enable me to cut the ropes that are keeping me bound to the ones who have hurt me. Fill that space with compassion and more of Your love. Give me an extraordinary grace to want to be like You in love and blessing to those who persecute me. And heal my heart, Jesus. Cover the places that ooze with Your tender hands and comfort my pain with Your precious words to me and about me. Lord, I also repent of the ways I have hurt others. Would You open my eyes to see clearly? Would You take away my blind spots? Would You enable me to put down both my victim mentality and my pride so I can look honestly at myself, so I can see how You see my broken relationships. Help me, Jesus, to forgive myself. I need You. I honor You. I love You, God who has forgiven me.

CHAPTER THIRTEEN

I Am Worthy

"Now if we are children, then we are heirs—heirs of God and co-heirs with Christ, if indeed we share in his sufferings in order that we may also share in his glory."

Romans 8:17, NIV

"The closer you get to the truth, the clearer becomes the beauty, and the more you will find worship welling up within you. That is why theology and worship belong together."[36]

—N.T. Wright

One year after the loss of Violet, I found a graveyard at the edge of town. I went to look for a place to bury my girl. I had no body or ashes, just her name written on a piece of paper torn from my journal: *Violet Mae Katherine.* At the base of a simple tree in the stretch of field that bordered the cemetery, I dug a small hole and laid her to rest. I covered her with earth and lay weeping beside her. A unique twig shaped like a cross lay in the grass next to me. I placed it on Violet's grave. I listened to worship music, and my sobs continued under a canopy of sheltering words. The pain of her loss, along with other painful losses of that year, came surging out of me. I held nothing back; every tear built up

---

36 Wright, N. T. *For All God's Worth: True Worship and the Calling of the Church.* Wm. B. Eerdmans, 2014, p. 12.

was released. As the emotion moved through me, comfort followed. Not resolution, but sadness soothed. As if my grief was a burn, and peace was an ointment. Yahweh was here, His "I AM everything" spreading and reaching into my "I am nothing."

Peacefully, I stood up from my place of despair. It no longer felt right to lie by the grave. Resurrection called me to stand tall in new hope. I began to sway with the wind as the music set my pace. I was singing now, words to Him and about Him. I was alone in this cemetery today. Not a soul in sight. This graveyard was now my Eden. I imagined my girls, Anna, Violet, and Krissy, singing the same song of praise and dancing freely in paradise. Before I knew what I was doing, I was running, and then I threw my arms open and spun around. I kept singing, and laughter bubbled out of me at the sudden awareness that I was expanding and exuding with joy. I couldn't believe what I was doing, only as a girl had I been this unencumbered. I continued like that, bursting with joy, until I was exhausted. I lay back on the ground to rest. I was both asleep and awake with the deepest sense of security.

I didn't want my morning with Jesus to end, but life called my name. Before leaving, I saw a beautiful ivory statue of Jesus in an expanse of headstones. He held a lamb in His arms. Of course, I knew this wasn't actually Jesus, but I had to get closer. As I walked toward the statue, I was entirely compelled, as if a magnet drew me. I climbed the three ivory steps without hesitation and knelt. The statue was so human, my breath caught. My tears came instantly, and I couldn't help but lay my head on His feet. The tears came harder, and I felt transported to another time, another place. I was so overcome, I began weeping once again, but the flow was gratitude and deepest love. This was my Rescuer, the truest Lover of my soul. I wanted Him to have it all, all I could possibly give, and this worship felt like what I was made for.

Eventually, I stood and turned from "Jesus." I felt sad to be walking away from this holy moment. I didn't want to leave this sacred ground where I had just engaged with my grief, my God, and gratitude so intimately. But then, realization dawned: *I can live this way! I can make every ground, sacred ground.* The statue had been a tangible way to love Him, but the risen and present Jesus was with me. As I got in the car to drive away, I prayed, "Jesus, show me what it looks like to live and love at Your feet."

In the days that followed, I couldn't stop thinking about the woman with the alabaster jar of perfume broken at her Savior's feet. She poured both her treasure and tears upon Jesus while He dined with a table full of Pharisees. She kissed His feet abundantly and wiped His feet with her hair. When the Pharisees criticized Jesus for allowing such a sinner to engage Him, Jesus chided in return:

> Do you see this woman? I came into your house. You did not give me any water for my feet, but she wet my feet with her tears and wiped them with her hair. You did not give me a kiss, but this woman, from the time I entered, has not stopped kissing my feet. You did not put oil on my head, but she has poured perfume on my feet. Therefore, I tell you, her many sins have been forgiven—as her great love has shown... (Luke 7:44–47, NIV)

This woman came boldly to Jesus, convinced and effusive. To come with such ample and willing love indicates that she knew she would be loved in return. Jesus tells us that this love poured out was a response for the many sins He had forgiven. This also means she was delivered from a life of shame, and for any remaining or future suffering, she had a Savior. Without a single word, amidst searing eyes, she praised Him with demonstrations of love and sacrifice. Without thought of reputation or cost, she threw herself and her prized possession at the Messiah, an act of deepest worship. If she had chosen fear of man, she never would've come. She was breaking many religious and societal rules by entering this home "uninvited" and interrupting a house full of prominent, religious men. But she didn't fear the cost of man. She feared the cost of not responding as the Spirit within her led. She was made for this moment. She knew it. He was the object of all her affection. She had discovered the narrow way in the woods and was forever changed. She understood suffering and sin to be a devastating, yet sovereign invitation to walk deeply into the heart of God. A heart where we will always be received and defended. Like the darkest forest embedded with the greatest of hidden treasures. Every step into the woods is an intimate step into the nature of I AM. Suffering with HIM is to discover Him, and that results in worship. Ascribing greatest worth to the One and only who is worthy and declares we are worthy. Through the prophet Isaiah, the Lord calls us "the people I formed for myself that they may proclaim my praise" (Isaiah 43:21, NIV). We were formed to give our love away to the One who formed us.

But we cannot forget our enemy. He preys upon our worship ascribing nature, and seeks to deceive and seduce us in the forest. He slithers and hisses and points out the forbidden trees in the center of the gardens of our lives. We indulge, we feast, and we rot. Our suffering deepens. We end up ascribing worth and value to the things of this world that cannot love us in return. We justify our lusts and passions and don't see the harm in sharing devotion and submission to another. The words of C.S. Lewis, recorded in his book *The Weight of Glory*, ring true for me: "We are half-hearted creatures, fooling about with drink and sex and ambition, when infinite joy is offered to us. Like an ignorant child who wants to go on making mud pies in the slum because he cannot imagine what is meant by the offer of a holiday at sea. We are far too easily pleased."[37]

We were made to worship the King of Kings. But we mess around in court with lesser nobility and struggle to make it to the throne. And when we do, we suffer more. The love of I AM is the only love that enriches within. This is the reason God said to His impoverished children as they fled a land of idols,

> I am the Lord your God, who brought you out of Egypt, out of the land of slavery. You shall have no other gods before me. You shall not make for yourself an image in the form of anything in heaven above or on the earth beneath or in the waters below. You shall not bow down to them or worship them; for I, the Lord your God, am a jealous God, punishing the children for the sin of the parents to the third and fourth generation of those who hate me, but showing love to a thousand generations of those who love me and keep my commandments. (Exodus 20:2–6, NIV)

This is the voice of our Maker urging us to live within His boundaries so we can fully thrive as He intended. God's commands recalibrate us to the way we were made to function and flourish. "Beloved, have no other Gods before me." The Worthy One made us in love and wants us for love. Jesus echoes God's words to the Israelites in a similar way: "Love the Lord your God with all your heart and with all your soul and with all your mind. This is the first and greatest commandment. And the second is like it: 'Love your neighbor as yourself'" (Matthew 22:37–39, NIV). These divine

---

37 Lewis, C. S. *The Weight of Glory*. Macmillan, 1949, p. 46.

decrees weren't rules to stunt, but safeguards to satisfy. We are so easily fooled into thinking that God's instructions keep us from good when, in fact, He is the only good. Worshiping Him is the avenue by which we are filled to overflowing with the satiating love of God. It's by worshiping I AM with all that we are that we become who we were always meant to be.

The apostle Paul is a beautiful example of someone who became all that God planned for him to be. However, before he flourished on the bread of life, he feasted on the best mudpies the world had to offer. He was "satisfied" by the world's kingdom, unaware that he was dying from poisonous fruit. God, in love, struck Paul blind on Damascus Road to open the eyes of His Spirit to the true King of Kings. This was a necessary suffering to reveal to Paul that he wasn't really satisfied at all. Jesus named this "new" man Paul, and the eyes of His heart were opened to a "Holiday at Sea," and mudpies never tasted the same. "Indeed, I count everything as loss because of the surpassing worth of knowing Christ Jesus my Lord. For his sake I have suffered the loss of all things and count them as rubbish, in order that I may gain Christ" (Philippians 3:8, ESV).

I am sad to share that in these years of suffering and pursuing God, I have snacked on mudpies along the way. I have responded to the enemy's whisper in the woods, "Come and eat." I have justified some of my unhealthy and ungodly choices by saying, "God is the one who gave me hunger after all. He wants me to be full." I tuck my Bible under my arm and feast on the world's buffet of streaming, consuming, and overindulging. I fill my belly with the stuff of life instead of the bread of life. I fill my plate with "Jesus and" instead of "Jesus only." And when I wake in the morning, I feel the hangover of the suffering I chose. How do we break our addictions to sin? Tim Keller says it both simply and strategically,

"The secret to freedom from enslaving patterns of sin is worship. You need worship. You need great worship. You need weeping worship. You need glorious worship. You need to sense God's greatness and to be moved by it—moved to tears and moved to laughter—moved by who God is and what he has done for you."[38] Worship is our DNA. Worship is our antidote. Worship is our forever.

The apostle John was shown the eternal fulfillment of our design in a glimpse of glory he shares with us in Revelation 5:2 (NIV), "'Who is worthy to open the scroll and break its seals?'" But not a single person, not in heaven or on earth or under the earth, could open it. John is devastated with sorrow, at hope lost, and he weeps but then one of the elders comforts him: "Weep no more; behold, the Lion of the tribe of Judah, the Root of David, has conquered, so that he can open the scroll and its seven seals" (Revelation 5:5, ESV).

John looks and begins to see wondrous, fantastical images of the holy elders and breathtaking living creatures. They are surrounding a Lamb standing as if slain. Yet, He is alive! John watches the bloodied and risen Lamb walk to the enthroned King and take the book from His right hand. At this moment, everyone bows. Harps begin to play, and golden bowls of incense, of innumerable prayers of innumerable saints, are poured out, like oil poured out. A new song fills all of heaven: "You are worthy to take the scroll and to open its seals, for you were slain, and with your blood you purchased for God persons from every tribe and language and people and nation. You have made them to be a kingdom and priests

---

38 Keller, Timothy. "Worship." *Gospel in Life*, Redeemer Presbyterian Church, 2008, https://gospelinlife.com/sermon/worship-2008/. Accessed 15 Apr. 2025.

to serve our God, and they will reign on the earth" (Revelation 5:9–10, NIV).

Then John shares with us the near unfathomable wonder that myriads of myriads, and thousands of thousands, including the creatures, angels, elders, and every created thing in heaven and on the earth and under the earth and on the sea, and all things in them, proclaimed with loud voices: "To him who sits on the throne and to the Lamb be praise and honor and glory and power, for ever and ever!" (Revelation 5:13, NIV).

This is the world's choir, and we are the voices along with everything ever created, rejoicing, celebrating, cheering, extolling, and praising all at once. This moment, established in time, is the antithesis of suffering. This is our jubilant forever. This is the moment we will know for the first time what being alive truly is. We will know for what and for Whom we exist. This is the moment we will feel consumed by the truth of how truly beloved we are, because we will see Him. We will see the One who died for us, understanding fully why He had to, and we will exude gratitude and love in return. We will know how "worth it" we are, and we will be loved in the way He always longed for us to know and feel it. Never again will we feel the weight of sorrow or the piercing stab of evil, or the unrelenting punch of pain, or the cruelty of broken relationships, the fierce blows of disease, the utter wretchedness of grief, the viciousness of abuse, or the emptiness and pain of rejection. We also won't be battered by our doubts, fears, and painful inquiries against God. And we will finally be free from the harsh attacks of the devil. The woods will dissipate entirely, all the gold of God laid bare. Living water will wash the residue of mud from our tongues, and the manna of heaven, worship, will be our only meal. We will be satisfied. This moment John reveals to us is what we were made for. This is life without suffering. It is the reward for suffering with Him on earth and friend… *it is coming!*

When we live lives of worship, we emulate this moment in our future, and we touch heaven, we taste fulfillment, and wings emerge from our souls. I don't want to look back from paradise and realize the life I lived on earth was less than everything He dreamed for me. I am spurred on from this perspective. I think of my heavenly family cheering for me. I see it in my mind, like rooting for Indiana Jones as he jumps, rolls, and speeds past every trap set before him. Even when he falls, I know he can and will get up again. We know he can find the treasure, and we keep cheering. From this vantage point, I am desperate to set aside every weight and sin which clings so closely and to run with endurance the race set before me, looking to Jesus the founder and perfecter of my faith, who for the joy set before Him endured the cross, despising the shame and is seated at the right hand of the throne of God (Hebrews 12:1–2).

We can listen to the elder's words to John in the book of Revelation, and we, too, can stop crying. We can look and dry our tears as we behold our Champion, our Worthy Savior. Life is so full of reasons to weep, but when we fix our eyes on our Victor, we can know that every moment of pain we endured on earth will be both avenged and redeemed. We will cry out with the elders and the angels forever, "Worthy is the Lamb who was slain, to receive power and wealth and wisdom and might and honor and glory and blessing" (Revelation 5:12, ESV).

The ecstasy we chase all our lives will be fulfilled in worship. Since this is true, why don't we access it as much as we can now, even as we suffer? I hope to be as impassioned as Paul:

I want to know Christ—yes, to know the power of his resurrection and participation in his sufferings, becoming like him in his death, and so, somehow, attaining to the resurrection from the dead. Not that I have already obtained all this, or have already arrived at my goal, but I press on to take hold of that for which Christ Jesus took hold of me. Brothers and sisters, I do not consider myself yet to have taken hold of it. But one thing I do: Forgetting what is behind and straining toward what is ahead,I press on toward the goal to win the prize for which God has called me heavenward in Christ Jesus. (Philippians 3:10–14, NIV)

What is the prize Paul speaks of but satisfied intimacy with God and satisfied worship of Him? In light of this, earthly suffering becomes a secret garden of treasure, an imprint of paradise, a sacred ground. We can hold the view that "Now all suffering that comes into your life will only make you great. A lump of coal under pressure becomes a diamond. And the suffering of a person in Christ only turns you into somebody gorgeous."[39] When we encounter Jesus in suffering, when our pain is comforted and sin is forgiven, we become as exquisite as the woman with the alabaster jar of perfume. We will take that which is most precious to us, our very lives, and we will ignore the whispering voices of the judges who mock in the court of the King. We will weep, kiss, and dry His feet, and we will soar to the heights we were made for, as sure as we bow low. Suffering is the sacred aisle unto the throne of God.

---

39   Keller, Timothy. *Walking with God Through Pain and Suffering.* Riverhead Books, 2013, p. 180.

"Child of worship" is the phrase I heard when I was three months pregnant with Anna. "Jesus, what do you want me to pray most for this baby?" "Child of worship" is what He delivered to my heart. This became my most fervent prayer for her. Then one morning, I read in my Bible about Anna, the widowed and elderly prophetess: "...She never left the temple but worshiped night and day, fasting and praying" (Luke 2:37, NIV). It was at that moment that I knew our baby's name was Anna. As I have reflected over the years on this phrase, I realize now that "Child of worship" is the answer to God's most fervent prayer for me. The truest answer to suffering is worship. Being a child of worship means staring with the eyes of my heart into His face on the bitter days as well as the best days, while loving Him and absorbing His love for me. Being a child of worship is kneeling helplessly beside my helpless child and knowing the Helper is always with him. Being a child of worship is holding those who cry from the pain of loneliness, unanswered prayers, abuse, and disease, knowing our Good Father holds us both. Being a child of worship is trusting that when the swinging bridge of faith seems to snap, I am held in the arms of a caring and conquering God who will never fail me. Worship is being awake to the seducer of this world and rejecting the mud pies that glisten.

How are you suffering today? Are you war-torn by battles in every realm? Worship Him! Even when you don't feel like it, worship Him! When your circumstances lead you to mourn, mourn with Him. Even when you have no idea what you are singing or saying, let praise tumble from your spirit. Deep breaths will find you here because you were made to breathe like this. When we name Him in worship, He names us in return.

When we declare, "God, You are the Redeemer," He responds, "Fear not for I have redeemed you; I have called you by name, you are mine" (Isaiah 43:1, ESV).

When we praise, "Jesus, You are high and lifted up," He replies that He, "seated us with him in the heavenly places..." (Ephesians 2:6, ESV).

When we declare, "God, You are Sovereign," He resounds, "...all things work together for good, for those who are called according to his purpose" (Romans 8:28, ESV).

Every sentence we give God, He gives us in return, because everything about Him says something about us. Do you long to know who you really are? Tell God repeatedly who He is, and you will encounter both the wondrous truth of I AM and "I am." When we lose ourselves in worship, we find ourselves in Him. The forest is dark, but the treasure awaits. Go deeper in the dark, trusting that the unseen path you crawl and weep upon is a hall laid with red carpet leading to the throne. Rejoice; you are a child of the King. Run to Him and kneel. Break yourself open at His feet. Kiss them and wash them while His hand of blessing rests on your head. The throne is most accessible and visible to the suffering child for "The Lord is close to the brokenhearted and saves those who are crushed in spirit" (Psalm 34:18, NIV). Are you suffering today? Open the eyes of your heart and run to the King. Your father is weeping and waiting for you.

Oh, come, let us adore Him.

Dearest Jesus, precious Savior, I want, need, and long to worship You with every part of who I am. I need Your help to do this. I have feasted on the mudpies that the world and the enemy have offered me. I need Your Spirit to lead my soul and my body into the most glorious possibilities for me on this side of heaven. My suffering and my sorrow tell me to stop. But my greatest chance for healing, peace, joy, and restoration will come from kneeling at Your throne. Help get me there. Show me the way to become a true child of worship. I want to know You and to be renamed and defined by You. I echo the words of Augustine of Hippo: "You never go away from us, yet we have difficulty in returning to You. Come, Lord, stir us up and call us back. Kindle and seize us. Be our fire and our sweetness. Let us love. Let us run."[40] Oh, Worthy I AM, I worship You. Come, Lord, stir us up and call us back. Kindle and seize us. Be our fire and our sweetness. Let us love. Let us run. Oh, Worthy I AM, I worship You.

---

40   Augustine. *Confessions*. Translated by Henry Chadwick, Oxford University Press, 2008, p. 138.

PART 3

To Be Well

CHAPTER FOURTEEN

I Am Well

"It is done. I am the Alpha and the Omega, the beginning and the end. To the thirsty I will give water without cost from the spring of the water of life."
Revelation 21:6, ESV

"Who does not thirst? Who has not mind-thirsts or heart-thirsts, soul-thirsts or body-thirsts. Well, no matter which, or whether I have them all, come unto me and remain thirsty? Ah no! Come unto me and drink."[41]
—Hudson Taylor

"All shall be well. And all shall be well.
And all manner of thing shall be well."[42]
—Mother Julian of Norwich

It is spring once again. I wrote words straight through fall and winter. The blankets were just as warm as I expected them to be, and the fire blazed steady and strong. Winter dazzled white with grace, even though snow didn't make its way to the Valley this year. Manna came instead. The birds that flew south in October have now made nests all over our May yard. I love these little baskets of promise, woven piece by piece with strands of

---

41 Taylor, Howard, and Geraldine Taylor. *Hudson Taylor's Spiritual Secret.* Moody Publishers, 2009, p. 167.

42 Julian of Norwich. *Revelations of Divine Love.* Translated by Barry Windeatt, Oxford University Press, 2012, p. 58.

earth, speckled blue with eggs. New life has come. The trees have dressed themselves once again in the most beautiful pink, purple, and yellow gowns. It's nature's ball, and the Virginia dogwood is the guest of honor. She dazzles in white and pastels, her gospel petals waving to me in the wind. She waves to get my attention. She waves to tell me a story—the story of I AM and the story of who *I* am.

I am well.

This week, I sat on a hillside, an outdoor theater, in my friend Pearl's yard. We looked out over our gorgeous Shenandoah Valley, and I had to pinch myself that we get to call this home. We were surrounded by vibrant shades of stretching and sweeping green glory. The sky was an ocean of blues with pillowy white clouds beckoning rest and wonder. I felt small and yet significant, dabbed onto the grass of this magnificent canvas of His. We sat with six other women from our church, sisters, and poured out our hearts, hurts, and needs before one another and the Lord. We ate buttery oatmeal cookies, and Carolina played notes and sang tunes. Together, we filled the sky with trust and adoration. As the sun set and our friends departed, Pearl and I made our way to the fire. It was smoldering, but as she tossed on something small and dry, it ignited once more. I AM was with us. We shared a lament that only mamas of children with brain disorders could understand. We shared suffering souls and swapped love in the presence of a flame, and I thought *spring needs the fire just as much as winter.* In every season, there is need, and in every season, there is Yahweh.

I climbed into bed that night, smelling the smoke in my hair and loving the scent of His nearness. Just a small ground flame, a burning bush, nonetheless. I gathered the covers and nestled underneath, snuggling into contemplation. I was ready to receive rest when a new cover was laid upon me, Psalm 63:1 (NIV), David's quilt, patched with verse upon verse of want, need, and praise:

> You, God, are my God,
> earnestly I seek you;
> I thirst for you,
>
> my whole being longs for you,
> in a dry and parched land
> where there is no water.

The pain and longings of my dear friends seemed to be stitched right into the fabric of the psalm. Yes, we were all parched, and no, the world had nothing to satisfy. He was the living water. He was the one we begged for, whether we knew it or not.

> I have seen you in the sanctuary
>
> and beheld your power and your glory.
>
> Because your love is better than life,
>
> my lips will glorify you.
>
> I will praise you as long as I live,
>
> and in your name I will lift up my hands.
>
> (Psalm 63:2–4, NIV)

Isn't that what we had just done? Lifted our hands and our confessions to the Creator of the canopy above and the clay within. The One who made both the heavens and hearts, the One whose love is better than the best in our lives. Hadn't we just glorified the One who allowed our thirsts, the One we trusted to pour and fill?

> I will be fully satisfied as with the richest of foods;
> with singing lips my mouth will praise you.
>
> (Psalm 63:5, NIV)

Six women sat on a hilltop and shared our hunger, our pangs for full wombs, full hearts, restored families, healed children, and freedom from anxiety, depression, exhaustion, and fear. And then, we came to Jesus. We spread out a feast of worship and ate until our deepest hunger was satisfied. Yes, we ached. We longed. We cried. Yet, we *believed* and for this reason:

> We were all well.
> Another well comes to mind.

Abraham longed for a wife for his son, Isaac. He sent his servant on a mission for a bride that ended at a well. His arrival was perfectly timed for the evening hour when women came to collect water. The Spirit confided in him that the woman who responded to his request, "Please give me a little water to drink from your jar," and watered the animals too, was Isaac's bride (Genesis 24:17, ESV). Rebekah offered water abundantly and showed herself to be God's chosen for Isaac.

Rebekah and Isaac had a son named Jacob, and he met his beloved, Rachel, at a well (Genesis 29:9). When Moses fled from Pharaoh, he settled by a well in Midian, where the Lord brought him his future bride, Zipporah (Exodus 2:17–21). The well is the place where God united His sons with His daughters. A place to come thirsty and to leave satisfied in relationships. With intimacy. With belonging.

Jesus longed for His bride, too. He came to Earth in search of her. When He came to the well in Samaria, He followed the footsteps of Abraham, Isaac, Jacob, and Moses. He came to get His bride.

Instead of avoiding Samaria, like every other pious, scared Jew, Jesus came directly in and headed for the well, Jacob's well, the one that greeted saints in the morning and sinners at noon. Just like

Abraham's servant, Jesus timed His arrival perfectly. But instead of looking for a pure virgin who would provide for Him, He came for an adulterous woman He could provide for. "The Spirit of the Sovereign Lord is on me, because the Lord has anointed me to proclaim good news to the poor. He has sent me to bind up the brokenhearted, to proclaim freedom for the captives and release from darkness for the prisoners" (Isaiah 61:1, NIV). Jesus found her exactly as He wanted her, a sinful woman with a severed soul, seeking men to mend what only He could. How do you begin a conversation with someone you already know and dearly love? One you knit together, stitch by stitch. A daughter you've been singing over all her life. A suffering soul you ache to save.

Jesus begins with thirst. He says to the Samaritan woman, "Will you give me a drink?" (John 4:7, NIV). But after a few moments, He identifies her thirst. Jesus told the woman things about herself that only an ever-present, all-knowing God could know. Regarding Him as a prophet, she responds, "I know that Messiah (called Christ) is coming. When he comes, he will explain everything to us" (John 4:25, NIV). Can you imagine the simmering in Jesus's soul and the smile on His face as He hears her words? She is anticipating and hoping for *Him*. Can you hear the rumble in His heart? He is moments from revealing Himself and capturing the heart of His bride. The one He knew before she was formed in her mother's womb (Psalm 139:13). The one He set apart from before her birth (Jeremiah 1:5). The one engraved on the palm of His hand (Isaiah 49:16). Heaven strikes its match. The flame is lit, the bush now burns bright with love and hope emanating and radiating from Jesus: "I, the one speaking to you—I am He" (John 4:26, NIV).

I AM.

At this sacred introduction, the woman leaves her water jar and runs back to town and announces, "Come, see a man who told me everything I ever did. Could this be the Messiah?" (John 4:29, NIV). We aren't told what the woman felt at this moment or if she said anything to Jesus. What she mustn't have felt was shame. If she did, then she wouldn't have gone to get others. Shame hides. No, this wounded and weary woman felt known and loved, and her instant reaction was to invite others to know the Messiah, and they came with her. Does this not say something about the way she appeared to them? Did they salivate with longing for what she now had—living water? Did they really follow the very woman they refused to associate with moments before? Yes, they did! Their souls were thirsty, too. After two days of drinking deeply of Jesus, the townspeople said to the woman, "We no longer believe just because of what you said; now we have heard for ourselves, and we know that this man really is the Savior of the world" (John 4:42, NIV).

We aren't told exactly what Jesus spent two days teaching His Samaritan children, but to confess Jesus as the Savior of the World must've meant they first confessed their sin. Jesus must've helped them understand what we hear first from Jeremiah: "My people have committed two sins: They have forsaken me, the spring of living water, and have dug their own cisterns, broken cisterns that cannot hold water" (Jeremiah 2:13, NIV). With the Samaritan woman leading the way, her neighbors were ready to abandon the world's water supply, to turn from sin to the Spring. They were ready to let go of their man-made cisterns for the soul-well and lasting, living water of Jesus.

God was just as gracious with me and my broken cisterns. On the night of Anna's seventh birthday, in a place of emptiness and despair, He was waiting for me at the well. Nursing baby Elijah with tears streaming down my face, I was dehydrated, soul parched, and desperate for living water. As I regarded my thirst, giving in to despair, I shut my eyes tight, shut the door of pain, and when I did, my spirit was awakened to Anna: her long hair swept down over a white linen dress. She bent over, reaching down, scooping something. As she turned around to greet me, her hand extended and she offered me a cup. She was standing in front of a well. I took the cup from her and drank a sip of what turned out to be deep satisfaction and peace, a sip that revived me. It was living water, and I realized I had not been living at all; I had only been surviving. As I looked up from the cup and back to Anna, I discovered she was sitting on the rim of the well, and around her small, pretty frame was the arm of Jesus. I stared at the two of them, Jesus and the daughter we share, all cozy and nestled against each other. I stared at them, and they stared back at me. Their gaze was one that held anticipation and joy, like I was getting ready to open a present they wrapped with a miracle tucked inside. The miracle was Living Water.

I opened my eyes, staring down at the sweet sleeping boy in my arms, my grief supernaturally turned to peace, lined with wonder. I understood the gift. I understood that I was thirsty and looking to worldly wells for unliving water. I needed the Messiah just as badly as the Samaritan Woman. My sin was different, but I, too, had forsaken Jesus. I needed Him just as Anna had Him. I needed more than belief in my Savior; I needed intimacy with Him. That night in the nursery, my eyes were opened to the well that was always there.

There is another thirsty woman whose eyes were opened to the well. We first meet Hagar as a young slave of Abraham and Sarah.

When Sarah tires of trusting God to fulfill His promise of a son, she demands that Abraham sleep with their slave. Hagar conceives and gives birth to Ishmael. Thirteen years later, Sarah gives birth to Abraham's son Isaac. In a panic to protect the birthright of her son, Sarah demands that Abraham get rid of Hagar and Ishmael. The patriarch gives in to his wife's fear and sends his mistress and firstborn son into the desert, with only a jug of water to survive. When the water runs out, Hagar comes to a complete moment of despair. She places her son behind a bush because she cannot bear the thought of watching him die. But God heard the boy crying, and the angel of God called to Hagar from heaven, "'Hagar, what's wrong? Do not be afraid! God has heard the boy crying as he lies there. Go to him and comfort him...' Then God opened Hagar's eyes, and she saw a well of water. She quickly filled her water container and gave the boy a drink" (Genesis 21:17–19, NLT).

The wilderness of Hagar is the place we find ourselves in when suffering ejects us into the desert of despair. You've been there, haven't you? Behind the bush, crying, wondering, accusing... *Do you hear me, God? Do You even care?* Please hear the compassionate voice of heaven spoken tenderly to you, "What's wrong? Do not be afraid. I have heard you crying."

Your pain is paramount to God. He is moved by your fears. He is moved by even our last effort of faith. He is before you. You may not be able to see today, but His eyes are a flame with love, his heart is lurching with compassion, and His longing is to save you. Like Hagar, He has brought a cup from the well to revive you. Can you rouse the faith, even the smallest amount, to reach for Him with a desperate hand?

I love the desperate reach of the bleeding woman (Mark 5:25–34). After twelve years of suffering and exhausting every painful procedure and doctor available, the bleeding woman is in a place of complete despair. She is resigned to a lifetime of misery, physically, emotionally, socially, and spiritually. Upon knowing that Jesus, the Healer, was coming through town, she says, "If I touch even his garments, I will be made well" (Mark 5:28. ESV). She found a measure of faith. She makes her way into the crowd, and she reaches for him. Touching the hem of His robe and feeling power go out from Him, Jesus says, "Who touched my robe?" (Mark 5:30, NLT).

Then the frightened woman, trembling at the realization of what had happened to her, came and fell to her knees in front of Him and told Him what she had done. Jesus, the Healer, Messiah, and King replies with the love of a Father, "Daughter, your faith has made you well (*sozo*).[43] Go in peace. Your suffering is over" (Mark 5:33–34, NLT).

Our faith is the belief that His dusty, holy hem can change our lives and make us whole. This is what the word well, *sozo*, means: to save and to make whole. The water from His well is the only living water source that can save a suffering soul and put us completely back together again. When we encounter I AM, He doesn't just rescue us in our suffering; He names us. When we reach for the hem of His robe, the cup of water in His hand, we reach as sons and daughters of a King. This is not a stingy Father. He is Abba, perfect in love and power. Revived by Him and His loving kindness, you, too, can stand from the ground of your suffering, sacred ground, and declare I am well.

But what if He doesn't heal my disease? What if I beg, scream, cry, and plead? What if I do everything I know to do to touch the hem of

43 Strong, James. *Strong's Exhaustive Concordance of the Bible*. Thomas Nelson, 1990. Entry G4982.

His robe, and still am not made well? I asked these questions when Anna died, and my Krissy did, too. True wellness exists in spite of sickness. I have made peace that as I delight myself eternally in the streams of His living water, I will be given an answer that far surpasses my earthly understanding, and I will be satisfied.

This stopping place here in the dirt isn't the end of your story. It's a resting place to hydrate, to drink continually, and to be satiated by the living water.

When I suffer in His presence, I come thirsty to the well. When I wrestle and worry, when I pour out pain and petitions, I invite the Living Water to fill me. When I reach in utter desperation for His robe, I engage with the power and compassion of God. I engage with Jesus' promise, "But whoever drinks the water I give them will never thirst. Indeed, the water I give them will become in them a spring of water welling up to eternal life" (John 4:14, NIV).

I love how David describes Yahweh, our Living water:

> How precious is your steadfast love, O God!
> The children of mankind take refuge in the shadow
> of your wings.
> They feast on the abundance of your house,
> and you give them drink from the river of your
> delights.
> For with you is the fountain of life; in your light do
> we see light. (Psalm 36:7–9, ESV)

David says that we feast on the abundance of His *house* and drink from His river of *delights*. The Hebrew word for delights is *eden*, meaning pleasure.[44] David is showing us that when we

---

44 Strong, James. *Strong's Exhaustive Concordance of the Bible*. Thomas Nelson, 1990. Entry H5731.

drink of Jesus, we are consuming our intimate beginning with God (eden) and our intimate and perfect ending with God, eternity, His house. If we fully surrender to Him, a pen in His hand, He will write the most sacred stories with our lives, ink dipped in intimacy with God. This doesn't mean our stories will be perfect or pain-free by any means, but they will be *Presence*-full. And *that* is the abundant life.

David also says God is our fountain. This is the love of God that erupts in the one who takes refuge in Him. We also see this fountain erupting in Jesus. In the garden of Gethsemane, He pleads, "Father, if you are willing, please take this cup of suffering away from me" (Luke 22:42, NLT). A cup that would flood Him with sin, drying up every bit of life within. From the cross, He cried out, "I thirst" (John 19:28, ESV). For three days, He was life-less and separated from God, and then, the fountain of God, Living Water, surged up from the ground. Our Savior drank from the cup of death so we could forever drink from the cup of life. When filled to overflowing, we, too, can run as the Samaritan woman into town and ask everyone around us to come meet the Messiah, to come and drink. We can extend the cup like Hagar to a dying son and speak the promises of God over his life. The suffering life is a gateway to a sacred life when lived at the well. And a sacred life overflows to a giving life.

It is fitting for me to end this book with words from a writer who has been so much more than an author to me. Ann Voscamp has mentored me from afar in the ways of grief and worship. She is a literal Shepherdess who has led this wayward sheep to the truth and tenderness of Jesus again and again. She has invited me to the well through many seasons of awful thirst. A favorite well is her book, *The Broken Way*. In it, she extends a cup of living water and offers the way to drink it, a life broken and given:

> The art of living is believing there is enough love in you, that you are loved enough by Him, to be made enough love to give. For God so loved the world that He gave…Is there any word more powerful than giving? Thanksgiving? Forgiving? Caregiving? Life-giving? Everything that matters in living comes down to giving. It's the presence of Christ who gives us every single gift. And the presence of Christ makes us into the gift given.[45]

To be well is to *be* a well, a deep reservoir to be filled and overflowing with the intimate love and friendship of God. I am alive today because of the many precious souls who have given me cups of living water and have brought me to the well. This book is my cup extended, an invitation to the well in the wilderness. May you hear His voice calling out to you. The still small voice that can be heard in the deepest crevice of the earth and the highest peak of heaven: "I will make you my wife forever, showing you righteousness and justice, unfailing love and compassion. I will be faithful to you and make you mine, and you will finally know me as the Lord" (Hosea 2:19–20, NLT).

Let us long together to know Him as the Lord, our great and glorious Yahweh! May you be satisfied, my friend, in the presence and provision of the Living Water. He alone gives definition to who you are today and who you will be tomorrow. Be sanctified in your pain. Be sacralized in your longing. Be satiated in your suffering.

Drink of I AM and be well.

---

45 Voskamp, Ann. *The Broken Way: A Daring Path into the Abundant Life.* Thomas Nelson, 2016, p.67.

Dearest Jesus, closest Friend, my Redeemer and King, I am lost, lonely, and dying of thirst without You. Take me to your well. Show me how to navigate the path from my mind through my fears and doubts, to my soul, where You are waiting for me. Show me Your kind eyes and Your extended hand. Tell me everything I need to hear and know about myself, all the ways I take cups from the world instead of You. Show me all the ways I dig cisterns that cannot hold life. I need only You, Jesus. The cry of my heart today is "Awaken me from death, satisfy my suffering, and invigorate me with purpose." Fill me with unashamed joy, that I may run to town like the Samaritan Woman, inviting others to come to You. I don't want to miss a single way You intend for me to both drink and to extend the living water. I am suffering today in ways that I don't even understand. I am wincing today from broken beliefs, broken relationships, broken abilities, and a broken body. You are wholeness. I need You, present, compassionate, resting, faithful, sovereign, powerful, peaceful, hopeful, truthful, forgiving, freeing, and worthy I AM. Fill me to overflowing, that I may till through all my tears and worship in wonder at Your feet, oil poured out and life laid down. Thank you, merciful Jesus, that You never stop burning, refining, and lighting my way. I trust You in this present suffering and in the suffering to come, knowing Forever with You is my earthly ending and my eternal beginning. Consume me with Your love in new ways and in every way. Take my every grief and show me Your greatest glory. Open my eyes to see You at the well, to see that You are the fire before me, and to cherish this suffering ground as sacred ground.

Acknowledgements

I wish I could craft a new word that means "thank you" in the fullness of how I feel and what I mean to express. A word that encompasses the immense love and gratitude that brings me to tears as I pen these words today. It's a humble, sacred thank you, and I mean it with all the tenderness and grace I possess.

Thank you to the many sisters and brothers who have crawled, cried, and cheered for me on sacred ground. To the nurses and doctors who have championed my life, hope, and healing, I honor and thank you. For my dearest family in Virginia and Kentucky who know the cruel crevices of suffering…what sacred encounters are awaiting each of us as we trust Him—our Way, Truth and Life. I love and I thank you.

To Dana Blauch, what would I have done without you these last several years? You provided me a gentle and grace-filled space to unwrap my wounds and to heal. You held the truth for me when I couldn't hold it myself, and you helped me to recover my birthright. I am valuable. I am loved. I am a treasure.

To Crystal Horning, you took the frightening word "intensive" and made it glorious. Thank you for helping me to uncover the feared possible self and to embrace my true self in the presence of the Lord.

To Carmen Laberge, you have encouraged and exhorted my story and my hope with such joy and immediacy. You are a sister like no other, and it is my honor to stand by the eastern-facing window of this world and to represent Christ with you.

To my love and my siblings who have walked these long years of suffering with me and helped me to articulate pain and biblical truths in a way that honors the Lord; Chris Kelty, Kristen Sloop, Dave Sloop, Melissa Sloop.

Thank you to the precious women who read these pages and offered honest feedback and a heartfelt recommendation; Pearl Hurst, Angie Strite, Kay Walsh, Melissa Sloop and Ciara Brennan.

And thank you to my gifted friend and photographer Chelsea Anderson.

To my husband, my beloved, we have suffered greatly together on sacred ground. You have given me what probably felt like your last cup of living water again and again. You have sacrificed for me, chosen me, and forgiven me. Thank you for believing in me and, more so, believing in the comfort of God that yearns to be released from me. You were so right, "There will be Joy." Your sermons are the overflow of your life, and you are my favorite teacher.

To Johnny, you read every chapter of this book and helped me process and pray through what and how to share. I cannot thank you enough for being my first and most important editor. Our very deep and real conversations have been sacred words on sacred ground we have shared. You are living at the well—drinking in dregs and offering cups to so many you encounter. You are a spirit-filled writer and poet, and I cannot wait to see how God uses your words for His world. You love deeply and authentically and I am so proud to be your mom.

To Benjamin, "I remain confident of this. I will see the goodness of the Lord in the land of the living" (Psalm 27:13, NIV). This is our promise. We are holding it tight. We are living in its power. You teach me continuously about the simplicity and courage of compassion and certain hope. You have the heart of a shepherd and the courage and strength of a lion. Your heart is golden, and I cannot wait to see what Jesus has for you to shepherd in this world.I love you.

To Elijah, you are light in the darkness, my boy. You shine brighter than the eye can see, and your purposes are great. Your honest words, humor, and hard work blow me away. My longing to know you is wrapped into my longing for more of God. What beautiful mysteries you both carry. Your patterns, thoughts, feelings, and actions are a maze that I joyfully traverse. Dead ends are only redirections to the deep inner workings of how marvelous you have been created, in the image of your Father. Forehead to forehead forever.

To Jonah, creative, captivating, intelligent, sensitive, heart-exuding boy, I am nearly lost for words, succumbing to delight as I think of you. Your soul is the deepest well, and I love watching God fill you as you honestly crawl, create, cry, laugh, stumble, and get back up again on sacred ground. You amaze me. You make me laugh. You touch my heart with your kindness. I love you desperately.

To Vivian Joy Noelle, as you grow, we see how perfectly the Lord named you. So full of life and joy. You are soft and strong in all the ways that remind me of Kristin Noelle. Your life continues to bring healing as I watch you unfold. My history heals as I marvel at the way you glow unencumbered. You, too, know sacred ground, my girl. May you know truth, freedom, and deepest intimacy with Jesus. I cherish you.

To my heroes on sacred ground—I am in awe of the truths you've harnessed in the midst of fierce storms and even more inspired by the life you've laid at His feet. Your honest and humble crawl is the most courageous trek on sacred ground to me. You're beautiful, and I'd be lost without you.

And to Jesus, thank you for Your perfect love that initiated all of this. I praise You for every painful yesterday and tomorrow captured by your perfect peace. Take this small loaf, my sacred story, and feed those who suffer with all that You are—Bread of Life, Yahweh.

www.ingramcontent.com/pod-product-compliance
Lightning Source LLC
Chambersburg PA
CBHW031512120626
46545CB00005B/1844